Godward | The Wilderness Steps

Godward | The Wilderness Steps

Spiritual Wisdom & Understanding

> *Blessed is the one who finds wisdom,*
> *the one who gains understanding*
> *Psalms 3:13*

Larry D. McClure

ISBN: 979-8-89228-168-3   (Paperback)
ISBN: 979-8-89228-169-0   (eBook)

Book Ordering Information:
Atticus Publishing
548 Market St PMB 70756
San Francisco, CA 94104
(888) 208-9296
info@atticuspublishing.com
www.atticuspublishing.com

Printed in the United States of America

Table of Contents

INTRODUCTION

The Great Awakening

Awakening – an act of waking from sleep, an act or moment of becoming suddenly aware of something.

In my book *Godward | The Prodigal Steps* I revealed that the greatest obstacle to man's advancement Godward is selfishness. Our self-will leads us to be selfish which leads to our separation from our source of energy – Spirit. Man's source of all energies comes from Spirit, and if man's desires are used only for self-aggrandizement and self-gratification then eventually his soul will dissipate and waste all its spiritual energy and lose its divine birthright.

To dissipate is to squander or fritter (waste) away. In the Gospel of Luke, Jesus tells the story of the Prodigal Son who after demanding his share of inheritance from his father's estate goes off and squanders his wealth in wild living (Luke 15:11-32). It was the Prodigal Son's selfishness that led him away from his home and it was only when he came to his senses and realized his foolishness that he finally returned home.

Selfishness is considered the original sin. Just about all sins can be traced back to selfishness. In Hinduism and Buddhism, Karma is considered the sum of a person's mental and physical actions in this and previous lives and the consequences that these actions have or will have on their life and lives to come. Basically, the Karma that we experience depends on how selfish or how selfless we have been. Every selfish thought and every selfish deed will eventually have to be met. In this life or the next. That's Karma.

In the book of Genesis, it was selfishness that led Cain, the elder son of Adam and Eve, to kill his younger brother Abel. As punishment God banished Cain to the Land of Nod. Nod, the land east of Eden represents wandering with uncertainty. Nod is the condition of "sleep" and if you haven't experienced an awakening then sleep is the condition you now find yourself in and it is in sleep that nightmares occur. The book of Genesis records that God caused a great sleep to come over Adam but nowhere in the Bible does it say that Adam ever awakened from his sleep (Genesis 21).

In the book of Revelation Jesus tells the church of Sardis,

"Wake up! Strengthen what remains and is about to die, for I have not found your deeds (actions) complete in the sight of my God." Revelation 3:2

The world has not gone through a great spiritual awakening and until it does it's up to the individual to bring themselves out of their slumber and realize the Truth and the only way to bring one out of material and sense consciousness is a realization of the conscious need to be at-one with God.

When he came to his senses, he said, "How many of my father's hired men have food to spare, and here I am starving to death! I will set out and go back to my father and say to him: Father, I have sinned against you. I am no longer worthy to be called your son; make me like one of your hired men." So he got up and went to his father. Luke 15:17-20 (The Parable of the Lost Son)

Of all the things in this world that we should be concerned with and aware of, is how damaging selfishness is to our lives; to the lives of others and how destructive it has been and will be to every civilization in the world. It's time to wake up to this alarming fact.

<u>S</u>elf<u>i</u>sh<u>n</u>ess is the source of sin. Eliminate Selfishness and sin is gone.

Children of God

Ideas are expressions of the mind. Metaphysically ideas are the minds offspring or children. Since all minds are a part of the universal mind then we are all children of the Divine Mind. God expresses Himself through ideas and it is these Godly ideas that form all outer manifestations. Thought is the movement of ideas in mind. Thought-forms are how thoughts are expressed. Before the manifestation of the physical and material there existed only thought-forms or the perfect-ideas in the mind of God.

Through the Law of Mind Action there is idea, thought and expression. The thought-forms (children of God) willed to express themselves and in their selfishness, went off to a place where they could experience their passions and desires away from the Father. Doesn't it sound a lot like the story Jesus told about the Prodigal Son? Jesus always told a physical story to explain a spiritual event.

Many of the early thought-forms or children of God found a place of expression in the earth plane but as they entered the physical realm, they became entangled in the material world. The children of God now trapped in materiality would have to learn the "steps" that would lead them back to their original divine position or remain imprisoned in a physical existence.

The earth would now be the "Plane of Application" or the testing place for the children of God to see if they are worthy to return home. Before they could be accepted back in the spiritual realm, they would first have to rid themselves of any and all selfishness that led them away from the Father. In the heavenly realm there can't be two gods – God and Self. The only path to return home is to become at-one again with the Creator.

The entanglement in materiality is still going on today. As God's children it is only through experience and applying our knowledge and understanding of God can we ever have a chance of returning to our spiritual home. This will not be easy and may take many lifetimes to achieve. If an entity dissipates itself too greatly through repeated lifetimes of self-indulgence and self-gratification it will eventually lose the ability to incarnate in the earth, thus creating a serious roadblock on its journey Godward. The sad reality is that there are those souls that have over time forgotten God entirely and have eliminated and banished themselves to the land of Nod, a place that's raving with fright; staggering with fear; where they are forever wandering with uncertainty, never to return.

"Then the king told the attendants, 'Tie him hand and foot, and throw him outside, into the darkness, where there will be weeping and gnashing of teeth.' "For many are invited, but few are chosen." Matthew 22:13-14

The book of Genesis is the story of Spirit-man (collectively the children of God) and its beginning as a "living soul" called Adam and his fall and separation from God. Spirit-man's separation or fall from grace was due to Spirit-man's misuse of free-will. Free-will was given as a gift from God so His children could know themself, be themself, and still be one with the Father. Spirit-man's free-willed choice of self-will instead of God's Will resulted in the loss of the divine estate.

As the thought-forms began to express and manifest themselves in materiality there was no suitable body to inhabit so they enmeshed themselves in bodies that were available becoming entangled in the animal and plant kingdoms.

The combination of the thought-forms powerful creative force combined with the lower evolved animals of Earth resulted in all sorts of monstrosities. Eventually, a great flood was sent to destroy these strange creatures. It's a theory of mine that the dinosaurs were the result of the early thought-forms mixing with the prehistoric reptiles. This is probably why they too were destroyed.

The Original Idea

The *"Original Idea"* of God was to create the perfect son – the Christ. Instead of letting God's perfect-son idea evolve as planned the thought-forms took matters into their own hands. For selfish reasons, like the Prodigal Son, they left their celestial home to venture out to a distant country where they could express themselves and feed their selfish desires and, in the process, they traded their spiritual powers for sexual energy.

After separating themselves from the source of love and wisdom the children of God's thoughts became distorted and perverted, and they abused and misused the Creative Forces. As time passed, they gradually lost all awareness of who they were and where they had come from.

After he had spent everything there was a severe famine in that whole country, and he began to be in need. Luke 15:14

Not all the children of God lost the concept of the Original Idea as some remained at-one with God. In the story of The Prodigal Son there was another son who stayed in his father's home. After seeing the fate of their lost brothers, the remaining children of God realized that the only way their rebellious brothers could return to their heavenly home was to realize their divine heritage and overcome their selfishness, make their will the Father's Will and become at-one again with the Spirit Force. But first they had to be freed from their earthly prison.

The Children of Darkness

Matter and material form is another example of the Law of Mind Action or expression of God. The material is the effect of a spiritual cause. As the material form, or earth began to become a place of habitation the rebellious children of God were drawn to the earth plane becoming a part of materiality, something that God never intended to happen. As the children of God enmeshed themselves in matter their consciousness became "earthy" rather than spiritual.

As the minds of the children of God mixed with the minds of the kingdoms of earth, they devolved to the extent that they only understood selfish principles and worshipped the force and power of "worldly" things. Their nature became primitive and their behavior animalistic. Spirit-man was now the nature man or the Natural-man.

Jesus said, "Adam came into being from enormous power and wealth, but he was never worthy of you, for had he been worthy of you he would not have died." The Gospel of Thomas v.85

Jesus, in the Gospel of Thomas is speaking to Spirit-man, who was made in the image and likeness of God and was originally created as God's heir and companion. Adam or the Natural-man came into being from Spirit-man's selfish actions which are not worthy to exist in the realm of absolutes and will *'surely die'* (Genesis 3:1-2). Spirit-man had transformed into the Natural-man and now the purpose of all religion is to reverse this transformation and return Spirit-man to his original divine state. Only that which existed before the Adamic Age will last forever and everything that came after will eventually end. It is up to everyone to make that transformation before it's too late.

He (Jesus) *replied, "Every plant that my heavenly Father has not planted will be pulled up by the roots.* Matthew 15:13

If an individual participates too extensively in a pattern of activity on a lower plane of awareness, the individual will become completely trapped in that lower state of consciousness and remain indefinitely unaware of any higher consciousness or ideal. These are the Children of Darkness or ignorance.

His disciples said to him, "Show us the place you are, for it is essential for us to seek it. He responded, "He who has ears let him hear. There is light within a man of light, and he lights up all the world. If he is not alight there is darkness." The Gospel of Thomas v.24

Darkness or a state of being unaware (ignorance) is a direct result of man's separating himself from his source of life – God, and the only way to awaken the individual from their sleep condition is through the realization of the oneness of God, and if this doesn't happen the only way to stop sin or falling short of the Perfect-Son idea is through death.

There are two states of death, the spiritually dead and the physically dead. The first death and the second death. Remember first in spirit then in physical. With physical death, there is still the opportunity of reincarnation and the opportunity to awaken but if spiritual death (second death) occurs the opportunity of reincarnation is lost as well as the opportunity to awaken.

Another disciple said to him, "Lord, first let me go and bury my father." But Jesus told him, "Follow me, and let the dead bury their own dead." Matthew 8:21-22

The children of God who stayed with the Original Idea were in a much higher consciousness and understanding. These superior beings offered themselves as channels through which God's love could reach their fallen brothers, bring them out of their slumber, lift them to a higher consciousness and return them to their divine position as God's children. The *"Sons of Light"* would show the *"Sons of Darkness"* a higher understanding and truth that only has its source in God. By seeing the Spirit of

God in action the Sons of Darkness would come to their senses and realize what they had lost and forgotten.

Jesus said, "I stood in the midst of the world. I came to them in the flesh. I found them drunk. I found not one of them to be thirsty. My soul was saddened by the sons of men for they are mentally blind. They do not see that they have come into the world empty, and they will go out of the world empty. But now they are drunk. When they sober up, they will repent." The Gospel of Thomas v.28

If a "living soul" continues a path of a lower consciousness of activity the soul-entity will lose its identity. The "spirit" of the soul is not lost as it will return to the Creator, only the identity of the soul is lost. This is what scripture is referring to when it says that if an individual's name is not written in the book of the lamb there is no memory of that soul-entity and thus no eternal life.

Then death and Hades were thrown into the lake of fire. The Lake of fire is the second death. If anyone's name was not found written in the book of life, he was thrown into the lake of fire. Revelations 20:14-15

Sons of God and Daughters of Men

When the Earth finally reached its fullness the Children of Light (Sons of God) entered the earth in five places. These five places represent the five races: red, yellow, black, brown, and white. At first, the Sons of Light were still in "light-bodies" and still at-one with the divine rescue plan. The Sons of God had entered through God's Will unlike the Sons of Darkness (Sons of Man) that entered through their own selfish desires. For a while the Sons of God stayed true to the Law of One, but eventually they too succumbed to their own selfish desires. Like the Sons of Man their thoughts became perverted and distorted to the point where the Bible says that *"great was man's wickedness on earth and that every inclination of his thoughts was evil all the time"* (Genesis 6:5).

When men began to increase in number on the earth and daughters were born to them, the Sons of God saw that the daughters of men were beautiful, and they married any of them they chose (Genesis 6:1-2).

The union of the Sons of God with the daughters of men violated the Law of One and now the Sons of God had also separated themselves from God; traded the Spiritual Force for sexual energy, and the plan of salvation was in jeopardy. God makes a significant statement here that will change man's destiny forever.

Then the Lord said, "My Spirit will not contend with [or my Spirit will not remain in] man forever, for he is mortal [or corrupt], his days will be a hundred and twenty years." Genesis 6:3

If you don't get any other passage of scripture you need to get this one. God is saying that man is temporary and once God removes His Spirit, man's source of life, then man's days are numbered. We don't know when man's time is up, only God knows, but if God said it then you can bet it will happen.

The union of the Sons of God with the daughters of the Sons of Man like the union of the thought-forms with the animal and plant kingdoms spawned terrible creatures like the beings called the Nephilim. These giants were very large and strong physically, but they lacked spiritual awareness. They were more concerned with increasing their physical strength giving little thought to the real source of their strength – Spirit. When the early thought-forms projected themselves into the animal kingdom they mixed the superior spiritual energy with animal DNA creating a genetic code that still to this day is passed down to soul-entities at that lower level of development.

I'm sure it was God's intention to send a great flood to eradicate from the earth this lower level of animalistic behavior in the consciousness of man. Like the dinosaurs, this adulterated creation had to be destroyed. However, the flood didn't eliminate it entirely. The story of David and Goliath shows that there were descendants of the Nephilim that still existed after the flood.

With the ability to reincarnate, death of these mythological creatures was doing them a favor. In their next incarnation, the giants and thought-form creatures were forced to take on bodies that were the result of the union of the daughters of man with the Sons of Man and not with the union with the Sons of God.

There is something that you need to understand before we go forward. The Spiritual and Creative Force is the most powerful energies in the universe. To mix selfish desires and destructive thoughts with this great force and energy results in gigantic problems, individually and collectively. Just as man should not mess with mother nature man should not mess with God's nature as well.

I've often wondered why God in chapter six of Genesis decides to destroy man, His greatest creation. The Bible says that God was grieved that He ever created man. But the story of the Nephilim explains a lot. The Sons of Man were headed in the wrong direction and if something didn't change, God's children would have no chance of returning home.

As man developed in the earth plane, he regressed spiritually creating a major stumbling block to his journey Godward. Man's thought-errors and false consciousness had to be stopped or all of God's children could be lost forever, including those entities who dedicated their lives to saving their lost brothers. The evolution of Natural-man back to Spirit-man would take many years and many lifetimes. Time is not a factor for God, but His patience is. God may be patient with man but everyone including God has their limits.

Life and Death

The dead do not live, and the living do not die. The Gospel of Thomas v.11b

Sin is missing the mark of perfection, the Perfect-Son idea, or the Christ. To counter this error (sin) death or the ending of the physical consciousness is needed. Death is just a transition from false reality to true reality where the individual has another opportunity to analyze what they have learned or not learned in their latest incarnation and how far they have come and how far they have to go to eliminating selfishness from their consciousness and once again become the perfect ideal son that God intended.

For the wages of sin is death, but the gift of God is eternal life in [or through] Christ Jesus our Lord. Romans 6:23

Death in the material world is passing through the outer door of consciousness into the sub-conscious or soul-memory where the individual can review what they have done in their physical activities in the earth plane. Then given another chance through reincarnation the individual once again has the opportunity to change or build upon what they have learned or what they need to learn.

God wills that none shall perish and gives all His children every opportunity to change and return home. 2 Peter 3:9

There is no way to measure how much time passed between the time the Children of Darkness entered the earth and the time the Children of Light followed. It may have been millions of years or even billions of years. If we look back at the ruins of past civilizations on earth, there have been inhabitants here for millions of years. And that's just the civilizations that we have a record of. The Earth has gone through many changes from the time of its beginning and the remnants of many of Earth's civilizations have been lost forever.

Many believe that we have been visited in the past by extraterrestrials, but the truth be known, that we, as the children of God have been incarnating and reincarnating here for millennia.

There are no aliens to God, all is One. All are God's children no matter what part of the universe they came from and although the so-called extraterrestrials may be alien to us, one day we will finally come to the realization that whether terrestrial or extraterrestrial we are all brothers and sisters and children of God.

The Chosen Few

For he chose us in him before the creation of the world to be holy and blameless in his sight. Ephesians 1:4

With the fall of the Children of Light, a new plan of salvation was needed. One nation would be set apart from all of the other nations for a special purpose, to restore what had been lost and return God to the mind of man.

This line of teachers, leaders, and lawgivers, would come from the line of Seth (*founded, set, placed*), the third son of Adam and Eve, and they would direct the evolution of spiritual-consciousness and produce a race of priests, ministers, and prophets who would instruct all men in the ways of the Spirit and lead them to the re-discovery of the Original Idea – The Christ. This was the beginning of our modern-day religious beliefs, rituals, rites, and traditions.

Through the lives of great spiritual leaders such as Abraham, Isaac, Jacob, Joseph, and Moses the plan of salvation made a major leap Godward. With their exodus from Egypt and during their time in the wilderness Moses gave the Israelites an identity as children of promise and gave them a new purpose and reestablished in their minds the Law of One.

Hear, O Israel: The Lord our God, is one. Deuteronomy 6:4

Moses made the Israelites understand that Jehovah was not just the God of their forefathers but was also their personal God and that He wasn't just some absent Father in some place far away but could be found if they only looked within themselves.

At this point in your journey Godward you need to ask yourself to whom are you going to serve – Self-will or God's Will. This has been the choice of every entity and every child of God that is in or that has ever past through the earth plane. We may for a season partake of the earth and all its forbidden fruits but one day that will end. As God told Adam, if you eat from the tree of knowledge of good and evil you won't be around to eat of the tree of life.

War in Heaven

While writing The Prodigal Steps something interesting was revealed to me. The Prodigal Son had a brother. The brother did not leave home as did the Prodigal, and upon his brother's return, he voiced to his father how unhappy he was with the way the father accepted the Prodigal back in the family.

"The older brother became angry and refused to go in. So, his father went out and pleaded with him. But he answered his father, 'Look! All these years I've been slaving for you and never disobeyed your orders. Yet you never gave me even a young goat so I could celebrate with my friends. But when this son of yours who has squandered your property with prostitutes comes home, you kill the fattened cow for him!'" Luke 15:28-30

Selfishness is not just a part of the physical consciousness but also part of the spiritual consciousness. Remember everything has its concept first in spirit and then in the material realm. With all the attention that the Sons of Man were getting, I'm sure that the Sons of God that remained at-one with God must have felt some animosity toward their rebellious brothers.

This may have led to the story of Lucifer Morningstar and the fallen angels. I would like to correct some of what I've been saying because I don't feel that the early thought-forms were rebellious, nor do I think the Prodigal Son was rebellious. I think they all were just curious. Just like the parable of the one hundred sheep I think the one sheep who left the herd did not identify with the other 99 and decided to strike out on its own.

"What do you think? If a man owns a hundred sheep, and one of them wanders away, will he not leave the ninety-nine on the hills and go to look for the one that wandered off? And if he finds it, I tell you the truth, he is happier about that one sheep than about the ninety-nine that didn't wander off?" Matthew 18:12-13

Selfishness may have started in the heavenly realm, but it is playing out in the earthly realm. In the story of the angel Lucifer Morningstar, it is said that he was so impressed with his beauty and intelligence that his pride got the best of him, and he desired to set his throne above God's throne.

How you have fallen from heaven, O morning star, son of the dawn! You have been cast down to the earth, you who once laid low the nations! You said in your heart, "I will ascend to heaven; I will raise my throne above the stars of God;...I will make myself like the Most High." Isiah 14:12-14

Unlike the early thought-forms and the Prodigal Son the story of Lucifer is the true story of rebellion. We also see this same jealousy and rebellion in the story of the Prodigal Son. The older brother was not happy about the return of his younger brother. Their father throws the Prodigal Son a party upon his return which infuriates the older brother. If Jesus was telling this parable about what happened in the earthly realm, then it also happened in the heavenly realm. As in heaven, as on earth. Apparently, some of the angels were not happy about the return of the lost children of God. This may be the cause of a third of the angels revolting with Lucifer and their expulsion from heaven.

His tail swept a third of the stars out of the sky and flung them to the earth. Revelation 12:4

The story of the Prodigal Son doesn't end with the father kicking the older son out of the house, but I think that is exactly what happened to Lucifer. To rebel is to rise up in opposition or armed resistance against an established ruler, in this case against God which the early thought-forms and the Prodigal Son did not do. They left without making threats. Unlike Lucifer, I don't think their intentions were to rebel I think they were just looking for a good time. To get to my point, selfishness can take two paths – self-analysis and self-generated pride. The former is easily forgiven the latter not so much.

Self-analysis is an attempt by an individual to understand his or her own personality without the aid of another person. This I feel was the Prodigal Son. He was just trying to find himself something I'm sure God doesn't take offense to. Self-generated pride is a feeling of pride in oneself; pridefulness and a feeling of self-respect and personal worth or what is referred to as the ego.

This was what the older son was telling his father that he felt that he didn't mean as much to the father as did his younger brother. Being the youngest in my family I too have experienced this with my older siblings as I'm sure many others have as well. By definition, an ego is a person's sense of self-esteem or self-importance. Although our ego may help define who we are and how we connect with others if it becomes overpowering it may destroy us.

Metaphysically the two sons represent two parts of our soul-consciousness or sub-consciousness. The older son who stayed home is our religious or moral thoughts. The Prodigal

Son is the sense-conscious with its appetites and passions. The Prodigal Son going off to a foreign country is the separating of our sense-conscious from its parent source or Divine Mind. If one believes in or acts through the senses (sense-conscious) then they see those who are religious as hypocrites and the one who thinks religiously sees the non-religious as rebellious and sinful. I've witnessed this in many churches I've attended that allowed a known sinner into the congregation with open arms only to upset many of their longer and older members.

Unfortunately, both thoughts exist in our individual consciousness and are always at odds with one another. When we unify our outer sense with our inner spiritual self, like the return of the Prodigal Son, there is great rejoicing. When the relations between the outer realm (earth), and the inner realm (heaven) are unified then there is *'a new heaven and a new earth,'* and the dead man of sense-conscious is restored and made alive and like the one sheep that was lost is now found. No wonder the shepherd and God for that matter is happy.

Jesus said, "If two can make peace between themselves in a single house, they can say to a mountain, 'Move!' and it will move." The Gospel of Thomas v.48

God can't allow any selfishness whether good or bad to exist in His kingdom. There is only one master and that is the Lord our God and as the Bible says man cannot serve two masters, for he will love the one and hate the other (Matthew 6:24). Until we again make the two at-one we will never enter the kingdom of heaven.

"When you were one, you became two. When you become two, what will you do?" The Gospel of Thomas v.11d

The purpose of this book and my previous book is to help you understand how dangerous selfishness is and how important it is to become at-one with God. NOTHING ELSE MATTERS!

The Next Step

Now that I've finished my history lesson it's time to get down to business. You now understand why you went through The Prodigal Steps, and you now have a clearer understanding of what you must do. The title of this book is *Godward | The Wilderness Steps*. Unfortunately, the hits just keep coming, as do the steps needed to return to the divine estate. Just believing in Christ Jesus is not enough, it's acting on that belief that matters. We must keep moving Godward.

Therefore, let us leave the elementary teachings about Christ and go on to maturity, not laying again the foundation of repentance from acts that lead to death [or from useless rituals], and of faith in God, instruction about baptisms, the laying on of hands, the resurrection of the dead, and eternal judgment. And God permitting we will do so. Hebrews 6:1-3

The Bible says we are to study to show ourselves approved (2 Timothy 2:15). The time has come to get off the milk and on to the meat.

We have much to say about this, but it is hard to explain because you are slow to learn. In fact, though by this time you ought to be teachers, you need someone to teach you the elementary truths of God's word all over again. You need milk, not solid food! Anyone who lives on milk, being still an infant, is not acquainted with the teaching about righteousness. But solid food is for the mature, who by constant use have trained themselves to distinguish good from evil. Hebrews 5:11-14

The book of Hebrews is traditionally attributed to the Apostle Paul but whoever wrote it couldn't have said it better. It's time to get off the milk and on to the meat of the story. Too much time has been wasted and we need to make up for lost ground. I've tried to give my readers more meat than milk. But I get it, some still prefer the milk. If you are the latter, I think you for your time, but this is serious business and not something to speak ill of nor to be taken lightly. Jesus had his critics as does anyone who pens their beliefs. Especially their spiritual beliefs.

As the Bible says a prophet is without honor and respect in his hometown (Mark 6:4). A prophet is regarded as a person inspired to teach or proclaim the Will of God and that is exactly my intentions – to teach those who are willing to listen, the Oneness and Goodness of God.

For my critics, I've have spent a minimum of 15 hours a week for the last 45 years in intensive research and practice on the topic of spirituality. This amounts to over 35,000 hours of study. If it takes 10,000 hours of study to make someone and expert on a given subject, then I would have to say that my life long search for the Truth makes me somewhat of an expert on that very topic.

But that's my ego talking.

THE WILDERNESS STEPS

Wilderness – *The multitude of undisciplined and uncultivated thoughts in individual consciousness.*

Step 8.	New Beginning | Reborn
Step 9.	Judgment | End of Age
Step 10.	Journey | Responsibility
Step 11.	Transition | Disorder
Step 12.	Government | Unification
Step 13.	Rebellion | Depravity
Step 14.	Double Anointing | Deliverance
Step 15.	Reprieve | Mercy, Rest

STEP 8
New Beginning | Reborn

New Beginning – *Letting go of the past and looking toward the future.*

Reborn – *To be regenerated, to be revived.*

Now that you have followed The Prodigal Steps and made it back to the Birth Line it is time for a new beginning. A time to start again and this time make better choices with your life.

You were taught, with respect to your former way of lie, to put off your old self, which is being corrupted by its deceitful desires; to be made new in the attitude of your minds; and to put on the new self, created to be like God in true righteousness and holiness. Ephesians 4:22-24

The time has come to leave your "old self," the physical man behind, with its limitations and temporal existence and put on the "new self" the spiritual man, who's abilities are limitless, and existence is eternal.

The Godward Steps

The number eight (8) is a New Beginning. If you have completed The Prodigal Steps, then you have arrived back at the Birth Line and it's time to begin again. You still have free-will choice so, do you choose again self-will and head back to the pigpen, or do you choose God's Will and move Godward? After spending time at the pigpen, I hope you now have a better understanding of how self-will and selfishness leads to sorrow and despair, so let's keep moving Godward.

In my book *Godward | The Prodigal Steps* you were introduced to some spiritual numbers and their meanings. These numbers are the movement of Spirit which I will be referring to as, *"The Godward Steps."* The first seven (7) steps are the first movement in God's mind or steps of creation. The Prodigal Steps are not part of The Godward Steps but are the fourteen (14) steps that detoured us away from The Godward Steps. There are many steps but four (4) major set of steps that lead to Spiritual Truth.

The Creation Steps

1. Beginning (Male, Positive)
2. Multiplication | Division (Woman, Negative)
3. Unity | Pattern | Establishment (Tri-Unity, Godhead)
4. Creativity or Creative Works (Material, Physical)
5. Grace (Laws)
6. Man (Lawlessness)
7. Perfection (Completeness)

On a special note, all of these steps are continuously in play. As you finish one the previous one still exists. God may have rested after creation, but it doesn't mean His creation is resting. The sun continues to shine, and the birds keep singing. Once you learn these steps you will see them moving in and out of your life and in the life of others.

The first seven steps of The Prodigal Steps are the steps that lead away from The Godward Steps and are connected to our bodily desires. The second seven steps lead us back to The Godward Steps by reversing the first seven steps. Steps 8-14 pertain to the mind as a change in direction and involves a mental choice.

The Prodigal Steps

	BODY			MIND
1.	Self-will		14.	Rejoicing
2.	Selfishness		13.	Reclothing
3.	Separation		12.	Reconcile
4.	Sensuality		11.	Return
5.	Spiritual Destruction		10.	Repent
6.	Self-Abasement		9.	Resolve
7.	Starvation (pigpen)		8.	Realization

The Wilderness Steps are a continuation of The Godward Steps after having completed The Prodigal Steps and pertain to the Spirit. It is in The Wilderness Steps that most if not all selfishness is eliminated. You can see why the church as well as the world is still selfish as very few have completed The Wilderness Steps. They are still caught in the vicious cycle of Self-will, continuing to go around and around in The Prodigal Steps.

The Wilderness Steps

SPIRIT

8. New Beginning (Reborn)

9. Judgment (End of Age)

10. Journey (Responsibility)

11. Transition (Disorder)

12. Government (Unification)

13. Rebellion (Depravity)

14. Double Anointing (Deliverance)

15. Reprieve (Mercy, Rest)

The Promise Land Steps are the beginning of the reuniting of the body, mind, and spirit as one. This must be completed before we reach the Christ Consciousness.

The Promised Land Steps

16. Established Beginnings (Love)
17. Election (Victory)
18. Bondage (Sins)
19. Faith (Fruits)
20. Redemption (Mankind)
21. Exceeding Sinfulness (Counterfeit)
22. Manifestation of Light (Witness)

Man is comprised of body, mind, and spirit and each have their own set of purifying steps to complete. By analyzing The Godward Steps you may have realized that the Bible is truly a roadmap back to God.

The Bible is basically in four parts:

1. Genesis – Spiritual beginning
2. Old Testament – Body development
3. New Testament – Mind development
4. Revelation – At-oneness of the body, mind, and spirit

Until this at-oneness of the body, mind and spirit is completed the three parts operate independently of each other. To be the super spiritual force that they were created to be they must function as one unit.

His disciples asked him, "If we are infants will we enter the Kingdom?" Jesus responded, "When you make the two into one, and when you make the inside like the outside and the outside like the inside, and the upper like the lower and the lower like the upper, and thus make the male and the female the same, so that the male isn't male, and the female isn't female. When you make an eye to replace an eye, and a hand to replace a hand, and a foot to replace a foot, and an image to replace an image, then you will enter the Kingdom." The Gospel of Thomas v.22b

As you can see making the three into one is not an easy process. It is a good thing that there are steps we can follow to accomplish this complicated task.

Back on Track

Now that you have finished The Prodigal Steps it is time to get back on track and continue The Godward Steps. The next seven steps are a transitory state called the *"wilderness."* The wilderness is the large number of thoughts in our mind that are spiritually undisciplined and uncultivated.

This time in the wilderness is needed to purge any remaining selfishness from our life and prepare us for the second coming of the Christ-mind or the permanent consciousness. I say the second coming because remember we are returning to God not going to him. This is not our first time being exposed to the Christ or Perfect-Son Idea.

His disciples asked him: "When will the repose of the dead come about, and when will the new world come?" He said to them, "What you look forward to has already come, but you do not recognize it." The Gospel of Thomas v.51

It is in the wilderness experience the Israelites saw and felt the presence of God. Up until then they knew of God but didn't know God personally. At this point on your journey Godward you too may have attended church and learned about God but may have never felt a personal relationship with God. If you keep following the steps this will all change. You may feel at this stage that you don't have the power to stop these false thoughts from entering your mind, but be patient, this too will change. The more Truth that's known the less thought-errors. It's like the light and the dark, they can't coexist. When the light comes on the darkness disappears. When the Truth comes the lies will be no more.

Man is a free-will agent, he may open his mind to the truths of God, or he may declare himself an independent and work out his salvation through blind experimentation. It can be said of mankind that we are in our experimental stage. In man's ignorance of divine intelligence and creative law (The Law of Mind Action) man has pushed the law of God to the limit and caused a great reaction to set in. For every action there is an equal and opposite reaction and the reaction to man's ignorance in the days of Noah was a great flood that destroyed the inhabitants of the earth.

Spiritually the flood of man's negative conditions has brought him dis-ease and suffering. It is time for man to reawaken and start seeking God and His divine law – Love. This obedience to divine law is seen in the life of Noah whom God spared from being destroyed in the deluge. Noah was the eighth man on the ark. Eight, as I stated, is a New Beginning. Noah represents the beginning of a new state of consciousness – the Christ Consciousness.

Sin

The Bible says to destroy mankind God sent a great flood (Genesis 6:1-22). The hearts and minds of man had become continuously evil in the site of God and God was grieved that he had ever created man.

The Lord saw how great man's wickedness on the earth had become, and that every inclination of the thoughts of his heart was only evil all the time. Genesis 6:5

Notice in this scripture that it says, '*the thoughts of his heart were only evil all the time.*' God was not upset so much with man himself but was worried about man's thoughts.

Man's free-will had led him to be selfish and his self-will had separated his will from God's Will (The Prodigal Steps, 1-3). Thoughts are things and through the Law of Mind Action these selfish and evil thoughts of man were being expressed and manifested in the earth. If this continued man's evil thoughts would upset the balance and harmony of the earth which was probably the real cause of the flood.

Even more dangerous is that man's mind is connected to the Divine Mind. If the statement "as in heaven as on earth" is true then the equal and opposite is also true, "as on earth as in heaven." This is the true war or the battle between the earthly mind and heavenly mind. Until both minds are made one the war will continue.

Heaven forbids that the earthly mind wins. This may be where that statement originated. I don't think this will happen because the spiritual mind is too powerful. However, the material consciousness is putting up a good fight.

Sin as a consciousness is a very material, combative and destructive state of thoughts. Hence the destruction of the flood waters. Sin is missing the mark or falling short of God's Divine Law. Divine Law is the law of God, the law of being it is the underlying principle of every man's being and of the universe.

Law is Love and Love is Law and to fall short or transgress this law is missing the mark – sin. Sin is the departure from the law of our being (existence). God's first command to Adam (mankind) was to replenish the earth and subdue it. Something that has yet to happen. In the book of Genesis God tells Adam to have dominion over the fish, birds, and all living creatures. These living creatures metaphysically represent states of mind that are contained in man's consciousness. Any failure to have dominion over these states of mind is falling short of what God commanded.

I would like to note here that this command is found in the first chapter of Genesis which represents the spiritual creation. I feel that this command was given to the Children of Light who were to come into the earth plane and take it over, which they also failed to do.

The "unpardonable sin" or "eternal sin" is the belief that God is the creator of sickness, suffering and death or any inharmony experienced by man. If this idea exists in man's consciousness, then it is abiding and eternal. So long as man believes that God is the cause of his suffering then he closes his mind to the gifts that God offers, such as: health, peace, and harmony.

Man's sins are forgiven only when he sees the error of his ways and opens his mind to the fact that he is heir only to the good. God did not create bad He only created the good and very good. Go back and read the creation story in the book of Genesis.

Once you cross the Birth Line and take your first step into the wilderness there is no going back. Crossing water is symbolic of leaving one state of consciousness and entering a new state of consciousness. Once this happens in mind it can't be undone. Once you know the spiritual truths you will never believe again that which is false and a lie.

For many years it was thought that the world was flat and that the earth was the center of the universe. We all know now that both beliefs are untrue. Once you learn the Truth you will start to see the earth and the universe in a totally different way.

STEP 9

Judgment | End of Age

Judgment – *The ability to make considered decisions or come to sensible conclusions.*

End of age – *The end of this present period and the commencement of the next dispensation.*

Selfishness

If there is one thing that connects every human on the planet it is selfishness. No matter your race, color, religion, political affiliation, sexual preference, age, or whether you're male or female, selfishness affects everyone. Selfishness (Cain) is the original sin and something man has yet to subdue and dominate. Selfishness has led mankind to be separated from his Maker and source of being. Separation is step three (3) of The Prodigal Steps which eventually leads to step seven (7) – Starvation.

To illustrate my point, that man's actions have led to destructive forces, consider what it says in the Book of Leviticus. The Israelites have left Egypt and are now in the middle of their wilderness journey. The Israelites had been living in the city, or Egypt too long and had forgotten how to live and survive off the land.

God, through their leader Moses, was having to retrain and instruct the Israelites in moral behavior and cleanliness. Egypt at that time must have been a pretty filthy place to live.

Listed below are some of the topics in Leviticus that God and Moses were trying to educate the Israelites:

- Eating animal fat and blood
- Clean and unclean food
- Purification after childbirth
- Regulations and cleansings for infectious skin diseases
- Cleansing from mold
- Bodily discharges causing uncleanliness
- How to dispose of bodily waste

The topic that was probably the most important and controversial was the topic of sexual relations. The Egyptians were notorious for their sexual practices and the Israelites probably followed their example. Below are some of the sexual relationships that God, speaking through Moses, forbade the Israelites to practice.

Such as having sexual relations with:

- your mother
- your sister
- a half-sibling
- your father's wife
- your son's daughter
- your aunt (mother's or father's side)
- your father's brother's wife
- your daughter-in-law
- a woman and her daughter or her daughter's daughter
- your neighbor's wife
- do not take your wife's sister as a rival wife and have sexual relations with her while her sister is still living

- do not lie with a man as one lies with a woman
- do not have sexual relations with an animal

You would think that everyone would understand the damage these types of sexual relations would cause but at that time in history they must have been common practice. These instructions were targeted at the males but I'm sure they applied to the women as well.

The reason I listed these violations or infringements is because in the following verses God says that if the Israelites did these things, it would defile them as it had defiled the other nations in the land.

Do not defile, yourselves in any of these ways, because this is how the nations that I am going to drive out before you became defiled. Leviticus 18:24

The most interesting thing is what God says next. Because of these sexual atrocities by the other nations the land was also defiled, and God said that the land had sinned, and it too would be punished. But look at what the land did because of its punishment. It removed its inhabitants.

Even the land was defiled; so, I punished it for its sin, and the land vomited out the inhabitants...for all these things were done by the people who lived in the land before you, and the land became defiled. And if you defile the land, it will vomit you out as it vomited out the nations that were before you. Leviticus 18:25-28

I hope you get this! The land vomited them out, God did not kick them out. This explains why the earth is so volatile, it has been made sick by man's selfish acts and eventually get rid (vomited out) of him. This too applies to the land you possess or your body. The body too will vomit you out.

This selfish behavior is what brought the flood and all the other upheavals on Earth – past, present, future. It destroyed the civilizations of the Atlanteans, the Mayans,

Aztecs, Romans, Babylonians, Greeks, Egyptians, etc., I can't list them all. Pretty much all the civilizations that existed in the past. This also applies to all future civilizations including the present. God said, *"I am going to drive them out before you."* And how is he going to do that? By punishing the land and making the land drive man out.

Judgment

The church has always used the "Last Judgment" in the Bible to instill fear in the minds of men and women thus compelling them to join the church. But for most in this day and time with the internet many are not easily terrified. They are seeking knowledge and enlightenment, not intimidation.

But you, Daniel, close up the scroll until the time of the end. Many will go here and there to increase knowledge. Daniel 12:4

Judgment is a matter of divine law. God does not judge as most Biblical scholars would have you believe, for it is the law that judges. Just like the land that vomits out its inhabitants that bring it inharmony it's not God that is passing judgment it is the land itself. Think about that for a moment.

Every departure or transgression of the law has its consequences as seen in the days of Noah. God is not waiting in some future event to judge you according to your sins. If the wage of sin is death, then by dying your sins should be paid.

And furthermore, if judgment is bestowed after death, then there is no opportunity to correct your mistakes. Unless you believe in reincarnation. But even with reincarnation the judgment is that you must be born again and go back and clean up the karmic mess that you created in the previous lives. Judgment is for here and now. Remember the earth plane is the place of experimentation and learning.

You would think by now that man would understand that he can't keep doing the evil things he is doing and expect everything to be ok. Even the Bible warns man that if he keeps sowing the same bad seeds, he is going to keep reaping the same bad harvest.

As it was in the days of Noah, so it will be at the coming of the Son of man. For in the days before the flood people were eating and drinking, marrying, and giving in marriage, up to the day Noah entered the ark; and they knew nothing about what would happen until the flood came and took them all away. That is how it will be at the coming of the Son of Man. Matthew 24:37-39

Remember at the time of the flood man's thoughts were continuously evil. Pretty much like man's thoughts today. In the present, storms are getting more prevalent and more powerful. We are seeing more hurricanes, tornadoes, fires, floods, droughts, and earthquakes. The more man defiles himself and the earth the sicker they become they both have no choice but to remove the problem causing the illness – Man. Man has made the earth sick to the point of forcing him out. He has made himself sick to the point of death.

What I just told you is on a larger scale but as the nation goes, as the world goes is how the individual goes and vice versus. If your thoughts are still of self, then they will have to be removed before you can move Godward or else you too will be vomited out. If your thoughts are not in harmony with the Divine Mind, then your thoughts are in error and in need of correction.

These selfish thought-errors are not founded in Truth and have no place in the absolute. These thought-errors, as Genesis 6:5 points out is from the evil heart of man and not from God. Before we can move on Godward these selfish thoughts must be removed from our heart and mind. These thought-errors have been making you sick and now it's time that you vomited them out. Maybe literally.

Affirmation and Denial

There are still selfish thoughts, false-thoughts and thought-errors that must be removed from our mind, if not we will never reach the Promised Land. When our thoughts are not in harmony with the Divine Mind these thought-errors must be eliminated from consciousness. To eliminate false-thoughts or thought-errors the individual must affirm the Truth and deny everything else. This is referred to as Affirmation and Denial. This doesn't mean to be in denial, but to deny thought-errors a place in our consciousness.

Just like the time before the flood men were going about their evil ways oblivious to the judgment to come. You too have been going through life oblivious to the fact that your selfish thoughts and selfish actions have brought a flood of problems to your life. But now you know and now you are the judge. It's up to you to pass judgment on your false-thoughts and false-errors and eject them from your mind and fill that void with the true consciousness.

Once Truth is affirmed in mind these errors will cease to manifest in our lives. By denying their reality we deny their power of expression (Law of Mind Action). Thoughts, whether positive or negative must have an energy source for them to continue to exist. No energy means no power. In reality, there is no presence or power of evil, there is only one Presence and one Power – God. Remember what God said, that His spirit would not always remain with man. Spirit is man's energy source of his existence. No spirit, no energy; no energy, no man!

STEP 10

Journey | Responsibility

Journey – *The act of traveling from one place to another.*

Responsibility – *The state or fact of having a duty with something or of having control over someone or something.*

Alternate Egos

As previously stated, the ego is a person's sense of self-esteem or self-importance. It is the part of the mind that mediates between the conscious (body-mind) and the subconscious (soul-mind) and is responsible for reality testing and a sense of personal identity (ID). If we don't identify with the True ego, Spirit-self or Higher-self (superego), then we come up with our own personal identity (ID).

It was our ego and self-will that led us to the pigpen and to our death or near-death experience. The Prodigal Steps that you followed were to return you to the place where your self-will and ego first came into existence – the Birth Line. To continue across the Birth Line with your ego (sense of self-importance) would be to continue in self-will. It is either self or God. You can't serve two masters. To help us continue on our way Godward we are going to leave our personal ego behind and call on some alternate egos to help us until we reach the True ego.

After following The Prodigal Steps, you may be at this point lacking self-esteem and may be struggling with who you really are. Once you've completed The Godward Steps, I guarantee that you will finally know your true identity. The alternate ego's will come so that you can keep moving closer to your destination –home. There will be many alternate egos appearing as we make our way to the Promise Land so don't try to suppress them. Let them be your guide and show you the way you need to go.

It will be hard for you to make this journey on your own and these, alternate ego's, will help carry you through. The alternate egos are higher forms of consciousness that can be identified in the characters in the Bible. This is why it is so important that you start reading your Bible. This higher form of Consciousness is called the Super Consciousness or Over Soul. The Over Soul will take over your life and guide you through the steps if you will keep self out of the way. The Over Soul knows what you need in your life, and it will direct things accordingly.

This is why you must not act on what everyone around you is saying. Be patient, the way will be shown to you. It is ok to listen to others but don't act to quickly on what they are telling you, sleep on it, meditate on it and ponder it in your heart. If the Spirit of Truth is in the message, then the soul will respond to it, and you will know in your sub-conscious that it is true. Remember the sub-conscious is the mind of the soul, but you can't hear its thoughts until you shut down the conscious mind and all those voices that are trying to get into your head.

If you're not a patient person, then this is the time to start. It is only through patience that we overcome time and space. If you are patient, then the answers to your questions will come. If you act to hastily then what you manifest may become a stumbling block and something that you will have to eventually meet and overcome. You don't need to be adding anymore karma to your life so go slow and be cautious of your actions.

Now that you have a better understanding of what the Bible means to the soul-entity and what it means to you as an individual, it may be more enjoyable to read. Just skip over all those who begot whom and start seeing yourself in each character. See if you can identify with them in some way, and if so, what was the outcome of their actions? More than likely your actions will have the same results.

The Call

Abraham is one of the higher forms of consciousness or alternate egos. Abraham is the *"call,"* and it is the Super-Consciousness and Higher Self that is calling to you. Christians will tell you that this is the Holy Spirit who is calling but in reality, it is the God in you (I AM) that is calling you home. Remember you are a part of God. If you are a spark of His Divine Light, then you are already hardwired with a GPS to give you directions home. GPS means God's Prevailing Spirit and it is always in force in your life you just have to activate it.

What called the Prodigal Son to return was his memory of his time at home. It is the same with our soul. Deep down the soul knows where it came from, and it knows where it needs to return. We often don't hear its cry because the world has busied our minds to the point that all we hear are the sounds of the world. It is only when we silence our self and let go of our ego that we start to hear its voice. This is why most people don't hear the call until they are alone at the pigpen.

When you hit rock bottom you find that the voices around you stop, basically because no one at this point wants to be around you which is a good thing because now you can start listening to your real self. However, the hardest voice to stop is that nagging voice in your head. This is the voice of the ego and why it is so important to rid yourself of your ego. No ego, no voice.

The True Ego

As you continue your spiritual journey you will start to realize that all of the alternate egos already exist inside of you. The Bible is not some fairy tale story it is the story of man from his slumber to his awakening. As I studied the characters in the Bible, I realized that all these egos were me; they were my thoughts. Some were good and some were bad. Some were constructive and some destructive. Some obeyed God and many didn't but each was fighting for supremacy and dominance over my mind.

Like the biblical characters, I was trying to find my way in this world but my true ego or my true self was being covered up by my involvement with my worldly activities. My personal ego was a part of the earth, but my true ego was a part of heaven. This was why on Earth I've never felt like I've fit in. I realized this is not my home. I'm still at the pigpen! The world knows you by your earthly name, but God knows you by your real name, your heavenly name and He was calling me home.

As I continued my journey the real me started to show its face. All my life I had only seen the natural man and now the true man the Spirit-man was rising to the surface. I realized that I didn't have to pretend to be some spiritual alter ego I was a part of the True ego – the Christ. All along I was pretending to be someone that I'm not or maybe I just never knew who I really am.

Jesus said: "You are pleased when you see your own likeness. When you see your real image that came into being before you did, immortal and invisible images, how much can you bear?" The Gospel of Thomas v.84

As I cared less and less about who I was physically and cared more about who I was spiritually the closer and the more real God became. And in discovering who God was I found out who I really was.

The Pigpen

The time at the pigpen makes you doubt everything you thought you knew about yourself. If I really cared about myself, why did I end up at a place where I was going to waste away until I was dead? And why if I follow what God says will it lead me to eternal life? Why is it to choose God is to live in paradise and to choose self is to live in pig squalor? The answer is simple; there are only two ways to travel in life; up or down. You may move from side to side occasionally but sooner or later your movements will be upward or downward. You either progress or you regress. You either move Godward or you don't move at all.

The Spirit lifts you and the world weighs you down and anything weighted is going to sink. There may be a lot of side roads but there is only one path or way home and that is to ascend Godward. The pigpen was the side road that you took when you got off the spiritual path.

Like taking a detour off the main road in an unfamiliar place with no GPS or road map, just traveling blinding hoping you will find a short cut to your destination. This is why it is called blind experimentation. Without God's Prevailing Spirit (GPS) we haven't a clue where we are or where we are going in life. But sadly, when you reach the end of the road you found a dead end and now you have to retrace your steps to find your way back to where you got off the path. That is the purpose of steps 8 thru 14 of The Prodigal Steps, to get you back on track and back to where it all started.

Jesus said, "Whoever has known the world has found a corpse; whoever has found that corpse the world is not worthy of him." The Gospel of Thomas v.56

You can choose to keep traveling the side roads looking for short cuts in life or you can get back on the main road to paradise. Once you choose the main road the journey begins. By choosing the main road you are choosing God. When you choose to make His way your way then that is when life really begins.

Jesus said, "I am the way, the truth and the life. No one comes to the Father except through me. ..." John 14:6

Jesus could have easily said that "I am the highway to the truth and eternal life, so follow me." Until we choose to follow God's path God has no control over our life. This is hard for some to understand.

God is not interested in who you're pretending to be He is interested in who He created you to be. God created you to be His child, His heir, and His co-creator. God may be amused at this act you are putting on and may even applaud your performance, but eventually the show will end, and when the curtain falls you will be left not knowing who you really are and where you really belong.

Until you give up your free-willed life and make your will God's Will then like the Prodigal Sons father, God can only wait for His son to return. The Prodigal Son's father had no way of knowing where his son was or what shape he was in. He could only be patient and hope that his son was okay and someday would return home. Lucky for us God too is patient and wants all of His children back home.

The Lord is not slow in keeping his promise, as some understand slowness. He is patient with you, not wanting anyone to perish, but everyone to come to repentance. 2 Peter 3:9

Free-will

Free-will trumps everything. Even though it sounds like it, free-will doesn't make you free. Only the Truth sets you free. Free-will just gives us the freedom of choice. It is only when you choose God's Will over your self-will that the gifts God has promised will be revealed to you. Until then everything that is in your life was made by you and all of the things you have made will eventually turn on you. Everything returns to its roots. All your selfish thoughts, all your selfish activities, all your selfish deeds belong to you. God doesn't want them He didn't make them, you did.

"Do not store up for yourselves treasures on earth, where moth and rust destroy, and where thieves break in and steal. But store up for yourselves treasures in heaven, where moth and rust do not destroy, and where thieves do not break in and steal. For where your treasure is, there your heart will be also." Matthew 6:19-21

The false thoughts and lies in your mind and heart belong to you and you alone, and they won't stop piling up on you until you stop creating them. The only way to rid yourself of these unwanted possessions is to deny them a place in your life, in your heart and in your mind. Quit hoarding worthless and useless thoughts. It's time to clean house and take out the trash.

Your earthly thoughts and possessions are starting to rust, and moths are eating away at them. Before long you will have nothing.

The Journey is your responsibility, alone.

The Exodus

Exodus (Gk.) – *exit; departure; going out; decease.*

The second book of the five books written by Moses (Pentateuch) is called the book of Exodus and recalls the story of the Hebrews (Israelites) as they departed from Egypt. The pilgrimage of Israel is similar to the Christian life. The Egyptian bondage is a type of bondage of sin or the bondage of the physical body; a place from where we must break free. Moses as a deliverer is a parallel or another forerunner to the Christ.

Exodus metaphysically means we must go into the solitude of the inner self and lead our flock of spiritual thoughts (Israel) to the back of the wilderness, where dwells the exalted One, the divine I AM, whose kingdom is good judgment. It is here in the wilderness that we are in training forty years, or until we arrive at a balanced state of mind. As for me, it took over forty years.

Metaphysically Exodus refers to the deliverance of man's highest religious and spiritual thoughts (Israel) from darkness and ignorance or the lack of spiritual knowledge. The Egyptian state of consciousness in the spiritual man is the body consciousness (mind of the flesh) – body-mind. When we cross the Birth Line, we are transitioning our body consciousness, material, and physical state of consciousness to the spiritual state of consciousness. It is the first stage in the process to be reborn. It is like entering again into the womb preparing for the new birth to come.

Reborn

In the Gospel of John, Jesus is approached by a Pharisees named Nicodemus who tells Jesus that because of the miracles he has performed he knows that God is with Jesus.

In reply Jesus declared, "I tell you the truth, no one can see the kingdom of God unless he is born again [or born from above]." John 3:3

Nicodemus asks Jesus,

"How can a man be born when he is old?" Nicodemus asked. "Surely, he cannot enter a second time into his mother's womb to be born!" John 3:4

Jesus goes on to tell Nicodemus that flesh gives birth to flesh but Spirit gives birth to spirit. Of course, this confuses Nicodemus even more. You have already experienced the fleshly birth and now it's time to experience the spiritual birth.

Like Nicodemus most people read the Bible as the letter of the law or literally. Jesus tells us that to understand God we must see all things as Spirit. Remember through the Law of

Mind Action everything starts in mind and spirit before it is manifested in the physical. So, when Jesus is speaking of being "reborn" he is not referring to being born in flesh, but rather to be born again spiritually. Jesus is speaking of being born again in spirit as if the flesh had never existed. Being "reborn" is just to start again – New Beginning.

As children of God, we were born in the mind of God, in spirit, and afterwards entered into the earth plane. This is a hard for most people to believe. Those who are still in the flesh believe in the flesh, as flesh gives birth to flesh, but for those who are in the spirit believe in the spirit – as spirit gives birth to spirit.

Jesus said flesh thoughts gives birth to fleshly things or physical things and spiritual thoughts give birth to spiritual things. One of the reasons for The Wilderness Steps is to transition your flesh thoughts over to spiritual thoughts.

So will it be with the resurrection of the dead. The body that is sown is perishable, it is raised imperishable... it is sown a natural body, it is raised a spiritual body. 1 Corinthians 15:42-44

Once your mind and thoughts are spiritualized the body will follow.

If there is a natural body, there is also a spiritual body. So it is written: "The first man Adam became a living being" (Genesis 2:7); the last Adam, a life-giving spirit. The spiritual did not come first, but the natural, and after that the spiritual. 1Corinthians 15:44-46

Once you understand that Adam and Jesus are the same one you will see the transition from Spirit-man to Natural-man back to Spirit-man. The first man is the last and the last is the first. Jesus, as the Son of Man (Revelation 1:13) had to undo what he had done as Adam or what he had done as the Son of God (Amilius). Each of us has to undo that which we have done in error.

Egypt

Egypt (Grk.) Coptic land; from the Hebrew name Mizraim.

Moses, in the book of Exodus, knew that the Israelites didn't belong in Egypt and started making preparation for their departure. This is symbolic of what is happening spiritually in you. You are getting ready to move your thoughts out of the lower worldly consciousness into the higher spiritual consciousness – The Christ Consciousness.

Before we can enter the wilderness or the state of transition, we must first, as the Israelites, leave the place of our bondage – Egypt. Egypt (Gk.) from the Hebrew name Mizraim which means *shut in; restraint; misery; tribulation; distress.* To leave our place of misery and distress is to overcome the world.

Mizraim (Heb.) – *Egypt; Egyptians; circumscription; limitation; bondage; affliction; tribulations; distress,* was the son of Ham, who was one of the three sons of Noah. Ham (*cursed, inferior*) represents the individual who has given their life over to sensuality (The Prodigal Steps #4).

Metaphysically Mizraim is man given over to sensuality and the sense belief that life as well as the individual is bound in materiality and is subject to all forms of errors that restricts (*circumscription; limitation; bondage; tribulation*) him from receiving all that is good.

Egypt was the place where the Israelites were held in bondage for many years (Genesis 12:10). Egypt is also the place where Mary and Joseph fled to save the baby Jesus from being killed by Herod. Metaphysically Egypt represents the realm of substance and life in the depths of the body consciousness. To the unregenerate man it is the land of darkness and mystery, yet it is essential to the preservation of the body.

Egypt signifies the darkness of ignorance and uncertainty yet has a special significance in the body consciousness. Egypt is the subjective or subconscious mind that is based on or influenced by personal feelings, tastes, or opinions dependent on an individual's perception for their existence rather than the Truth. Egypt is also referred to as the flesh consciousness.

In the sub-conscious (soul mind) exists both the spiritual conscious (Super Consciousness) and the physical conscious. It is made up of both spiritual and physical thoughts and beliefs. It is the realm of higher truths and falsehood.

For most of us this hidden realm within is obscured yet it is a great kingdom, and its king is Pharaoh, ruler of the sun. Pharaoh was the hard hearted who would not *'let my people go'*, but we should not forget that in Egypt is where we find the *"grain"* or substance required to sustain the man.

Now there was a great famine in the land, and Abram (Abraham) *went down to Egypt to live there for a while because the famine was so severe.* Genesis 12:10

The various plagues brought upon the Egyptians by the Lord through Moses are symbolical representations of what occurs when the ruling intelligence (Pharaoh) opposes the influx of higher truths. When speaking to others about the spiritual truths I've found that for most it causes them pain, many have said that what I was telling them was causing their head to hurt. This is a sign that their sense-thoughts are rejecting the spiritual truth. Like Pharaoh, it is hard for many to let go of their thought-errors and false beliefs, so they, like Pharaoh harden their hearts against you.

Parallels to the ten plagues may be found in man's various bodily dis-eases. The bloody waters, frogs, lice, files, boils, hail, locusts, darkness, and death of the first-born may all be found in the various dis-eases of bowels, kidneys, and other organs of the body. Most of these ailments are the result of our mental resistance to spiritual consciousness.

When the spiritual man reawakens, he realizes that all along he has possessed the word of Truth and when he begins to make use of it the result is an influx of intelligence (light) and understanding – enlightenment. As one person I know when awakened to the Truth said, "I get it." This is what you could say is "enlightenment" or when you finally understand the Truth.

As the person becomes more "enlightened," the darkness (mortality) begins to fade from their consciousness. Mortality, which is synonymous with darkness, decreases as the light increases until, as the Apostle Paul says, mortality is swallowed up in immortality and death is swallowed up in victory. This first has to happen in the mind, then in the body.

When the perishable has been clothed with the imperishable, and the mortal with immortality, then the saying that is written is true: "Death has been swallowed up in victory." 1 Corinthians 15:54

Egyptians or natives of Egypt signify sense thoughts, or thoughts that pertain to the unweakened state of consciousness. I'm sure once the Israelites were finally awakened, they realized that Egypt was not their home.

The Pharaoh-ego

Pharaoh (Heb. for Egypt) – *the king, the Ra, the sun.*

Egypt is the land of darkness (ignorance) and mystery and Pharaoh is its king. In the body-consciousness it lies deep in the hidden realm of consciousness. Egypt is the state of the unknown, a place difficult to understand (obscurity). Egypt is the material consciousness, the sense consciousness, the flesh consciousness, and Pharaoh is its king. Although obscured it is still a great kingdom. Metaphysically Pharaoh represents the whole-body consciousness.

Moses and Pharaoh represent two forces at work in man's body-consciousness. Moses represents the evolving force of new ideas that are pulling at the old states of mental limitations and material ignorance trying to raise them to a higher expression in life. Pharaoh represents the force that rules the material body or the fleshly body. As you go forward these two forces will be constantly at work in your consciousness, one holding on to the old material ideas and one idealizing new spiritual ideas. One trying to keep you in material bondage and the other trying to free you from it. As the Apostle Paul points out this struggle is between the flesh (body-consciousness) and Spirit.

This I say then, walk in the Spirit, and ye shall not fulfil the flesh. For the flesh lusteth against the Spirit, and the Spirit against the flesh and these are contrary the one to the other ... Galatians 5:16-17 (KJV)

Don't get discouraged if you feel that things are moving to slow let the struggle play out, Spirit will eventually overcome the flesh. For years I was back and forth living in the world and then going to church trying to make sense of life. I felt many times in my spiritual journey that I was off track and not making progress. Be patient the suffering will end, and all will be restored.

And the God of all grace who called you to His eternal glory in Christ, after you have suffered a little while, will Himself restore you and make you strong, firm and steadfast. 1 Peter 5:10

The children of Israel are the Spiritual thoughts that have gone down into Egypt, (subconscious) to raise it to the higher Super Consciousness. The subconscious mind gets spiritual inspiration from the Super Conscious Mind and this spiritual inspiration must be passed along to the conscious mind (body-mind) and lift it to a higher level of understanding. Remember the body-mind or conscious mind is the flesh consciousness and the sense consciousness. The goal of the unregenerate man is to raise the whole body: mind, soul and body to the Christ Consciousness and the subconscious mind (soul) plays an important part in this process.

The reason for the slow pace is that the Spirit Consciousness is so powerful that if it instantly changed your thoughts, it would be too overwhelming for the body and would probably destroy it. For most the new spiritual ideas are too painful for their minds. Remember I told you about those of whom I was sharing this information said that it made their heads hurt.

These spiritual thoughts must have time in Egypt to gradually set up the circumstances that will free you from the grasp of Pharaoh – the material consciousness.

"And no one pours new wine into old wineskins. If he does, the new wine will burst the skins, the wine will run out and the wineskins will be ruined. No new wine must be poured in new wineskins." Luke 5:37-38

Pharaoh represents a part of the ego that must be given up. When you start putting demands on your Pharaoh-ego, in fear of losing you Pharaoh hardens his heart against you. Sometimes it might be you that hardens your heart or it may be someone else who hardens their heart against you, but either way it has to happen before you can start your transition from the temporal to the permanent.

For me there were many people and things I needed to let go, but most of them I was unwilling to part with. So, they hardened their hearts against me. I lost my job, my girlfriend, my son, some friends and even family members. It was painful at the time but like the scripture says in 1 Peter, I am now stronger physically and spiritually, and just about all that I gave up or gave me up has been restored. So don't get discouraged when you start losing things if you don't let them go or if they don't let you go then you may never see the Promised Land.

The Israelites

Israel (Heb.) – *contending for God; striving for God; domination with God; a prince of God; domination with God; rulership with God.*

The Israelites are the descendants of Jacob (Israel), the son of Isaac and Rebekah and grandson of Abraham *(father of a multitude)*. Metaphysically the Israelites represent our religious thoughts in consciousness, which are undergoing spiritual discipline. On our journey from sense consciousness to the permanent spiritual consciousness, or from Egypt to the Promised Land, all of our religious thoughts (multitude of thoughts) must reawaken to Spiritual Truth.

The Israelites are our spiritual thoughts and their purpose in the natural man's mind is to bring his body-consciousness out of sense consciousness and lift it up to the higher Super Consciousness or Christ Consciousness.

Israel, as an idea of development, is the result of the struggle to overcome or prevail over something of difficulty. We are all Israel for we all struggle to overcome the world and to do that we must first overcome our self and our selfish nature.

Following The Prodigal Steps has helped us find ourselves and helped us understand the role selfishness has played in causing dis-ease in our life. The Prodigal Steps may have made us realize that self is our worse enemy, but there is still that chance we didn't learn from our trip to the pigpen and may again return to our old life and its pain and despair. It would be foolish to have spent all our time and energy following The Prodigal Steps just to go back through them again and again. Like the dog that returns to his vomit why would you want to return to what made you sick and almost killed you?

As a dog returns to its vomit, so a fool repeats his folly. Proverbs 26:11

Folly is the lack of good sense or foolishness. In a biblical sense, folly is to feel that seeking the Truth is not a worthy pursuit and that it is better for one to follow their own path and make their own destiny. The Prodigal Son followed his own path, and it led him to the pigpen and starvation. We must continue to move forward and not look back. Remember the fate of Lot's wife (Genesis 19). She was told to leave her home of Sodom and Gomorrah and to not look back, but she had to have one last look at her previous life before she left, and she ended up turning to a pillar of salt.

If you are journeying from place to place, counting on the past and looking to the future and found no satisfaction in life then change your attitude to that symbolized by Israel and find peace in God's reality (*rulership with God*). Israel represents the reality of spiritual ideas in consciousness. Israel (*a prince of God*) represents the man whose consciousness is founded in Spiritual Truth – Spiritual Consciousness or Christ Consciousness

To fully understand the spiritualization of the natural man requires the study in the Bible of Abraham to Jesus. From Abraham, the "calling" of a higher understanding to the realization of that higher understanding – Christ Jesus. The unfoldment and lifting into full Spiritual Consciousness include the body of man, which must be unified with mind and spirit (soul), that it may take on and manifest the true spiritual image (substance and character) of God that God idealized in the beginning – The Christ, the Perfect-Son idea. In mind, body and spirit (soul) each of us must come into the perfect expression and likeness of God.

And just as we have borne the likeness of the earthly man, so shall we [so let us] bear the likeness of the man from heaven. 1 Corinthians 15:49

In selfishness only oneself is expressed and why it is a sin or missing the mark of perfection. Self is always missing the mark (sin) until it hits the mark of perfection – The Christ. The Perfect-Son idea.

Be perfect, therefore, as your heavenly Father is perfect. Matthew 5:48

When our personal will (self-will) doesn't recognize that the Christ Consciousness should rule our mind then our lives aren't guided by love and wisdom, and we become stubborn in our thoughts refusing to change our opinions and chosen course of action. This is selfishness.

Our selfish actions always bring trouble upon ourselves leading to our separation from others, to feeding our senses, to belittling or humiliating (self-abasement) our self to the point of starvation and death (the pigpen). The uplifting and redeeming of the entire man will not be complete until the natural man is born again of Spirit and the Christ, the Perfect-Son idea, comes to perfection.

It is through Spirit within us, the Christ or real self (I AM) that the intellect is quickened, and Truth is established in consciousness. Jesus is the only one of whom I know that brought the Christ or Perfect-Son idea into fruition.

…And a voice came from heaven: "You are my Son, whom I love; with you I am well pleased." Luke 3:22

At least we have an example to follow.

The Moses-ego

Moses (Heb.) – *drawing out; drawer out; drawing forth; extracting, i.e., from the water; water saved.*

Four-hundred-year cycles play a recurrent part in the spiritual history of Israel. When the book of Exodus opens, the four-hundred-year period of captivity foretold to Abraham is nearly completed. An identical time span occurs between the Old Testament and the New Testament. As the Israelites cried out to God in times of distress great leaders were sent to guide them and return them to their godly path. Moses was one of those leaders and his story dominates most of the Old Testament.

Moses was born a Hebrew or what the Egyptians called the Israelites. Although born a Hebrew he was raised an Egyptian. Like Joseph, the son of Jacob and Rachel, Moses may have been born in poverty, but he was raised in the lap of luxury. The biblical story records that Pharaoh's daughter found the child Moses in a basket floating on the Nile River. The child was immediately taken into Egyptian court and raised as Egyptian. It is said that Moses true mother was hired as his nurse, and he may have spent several years of his life in his own home and among his own people. When Moses was older, he went to live as the son of Pharaoh's daughter.

Moses' name means to "draw out" and that is what the Moses-ego is going to do for you, draw you out of the material world. Like Moses, we are being raised in an alien place, but the difference is that although we were born in luxury (heaven) we are being raised in poverty (earth).

Jesus said, "If flesh come into being because of spirit, it is wonderful. If spirit came into being because of the body, it is exceedingly wonderful. I am amazed that this great wealth has appeared in poverty." The Gospel of Thomas v.29

As children of God, we were born in a heavenly place, and like the Prodigal Son left our home to make our own destiny. No matter how we try we will never be comfortable living away from our original home. For Moses this was true as well and he couldn't stop remembering who it was that mothered him as a child.

The birth of Moses represents man's development in consciousness of the law of being for our negative side. Water represents universal negation, and it also represents great possibilities (*extracting from the water; water-saved*). It is seemingly out of our negative conditions that we find new spiritual growth. It is when we are in Egyptian darkness and in a weakened watery state that we are in a perfect position for the higher understanding of Truth. This is also true of the pigpen, a place where we are also living in a weakened and negative state.

Truth in its infancy must be protected and surrounded by love and trust, just as the baby Moses was lovingly placed in a basket (ark) by his mother who trusted that this ark would carry her child over the waters of negation to place where her child would have a better life. You too must believe that you are going to a better place and to a better life.

As the Moses-ego grows within, you will become zealous for the fundamental truth developing in your mind. You will do anything to protect these new spiritual thoughts, even to the point of destroying whatever opposes them. After completing The Prodigal Steps, you are now more aware of these spiritual truths. You now "get it" and have a better understanding of spiritual things. They are now a part of your consciousness and you're not ready to give them up. So, you will do whatever it takes to defend them. And defend them you will.

In Exodus 2:11-12 it is recorded that Moses saw the oppression of his brethren, the Hebrews, and kills an Egyptian taskmaster after he sees him beat one of the Hebrew slaves. According to Egyptian law, Moses should not have taken the Hebrews side. It is said of Moses that he had a violent temper but his taking the side of the Hebrew shows that his sympathies were with the Hebrews.

Because Moses was seen as an Egyptian the Hebrews resented Moses and taunted him with their knowledge of the slaying even though Moses was defending one of them. This is the attitude of many today who are in bondage and yet resent any interference and taunt those who are trying to escape with memories of their past sins. If you read some of the comments on-line of my book, you will see that this is true for me as well. It was probably one of the Hebrews who told Pharaoh about the murder; someone who had no more understanding of Moses' purpose than the one who disputed with him.

Someone that has no understanding of your newfound purpose will also taunt and try to provoke you to anger. Those who are still in the dark have no understanding of the truth.

Jesus said, "I tell my mysteries to people worthy of my mysteries." The Gospel of Thomas v.62a

They will mock you and try to trip you up. Don't listen to them. The Bible says not to give holy things to dogs nor cast pearls to swine.

"Do not give dogs what is sacred; do not throw your pearls to pigs. If you do, they may trample them under their feet, and then turn and tear you to pieces." Matthew 7:6

To the Hebrews, Moses was an Egyptian. They didn't know he was really a Hebrew who wanted to help his people. The incident happened so fast they never knew the real reason for the slaying.

A different story related to this incident says that a daughter of the princess Hatshepsut, a sister of Moses, was pledged to one of the leaders of Israel, in the house of Levi; and was raped by an Egyptian. It was this same Egyptian that Moses killed in anger. Although Moses may have had a good reason to kill the Egyptian his anger and his taking a life is not to be condoned. This killing by Egyptian law was punishable by death and led Moses to flee to a place where there could be the further unfolding of his consciousness, and of his destiny.

Moses flight from Egypt took him to the land of Midian, where he married into the household of Reul, a priest of that land (Exodus 2:15-22).

Like Moses those of whom I was trying to help also turned on me. They were not ready to hear the Truth, so I too fled to a place of isolation to deal with my anger. This will happen to you as well. Remember those who are at the pigpen or on their way there must come to their own realization of their error and learn for themselves. Their Pharaoh-ego is still in charge, and it will not let someone else tell it what to do. At this point in your journey, it is not the time or place to intervene in the lives of others. You still have your own problems to deal with.

The Hebrews are thoughts that have come up out of the purely material and passed over to a higher concept of God and of His laws. You now are beginning to have a clearer and closer relationship with the Creator, but these higher thoughts are still in their infancy and still under the law and will not mature until you reach the highest consciousness, the Christ Consciousness. Egyptian or sense-thoughts, whether they are your thoughts or the thoughts of others, try to beat down these new higher spiritual thoughts. These sense-thoughts must be stopped as Moses stopped the Egyptian beating the Hebrew. Let's be clear here, we are talking about spiritual thoughts as opposed to sense-thoughts. Don't think I'm saying to kill anyone who opposes your higher thoughts. We are speaking metaphorically and metaphysically.

In the book of Revelation Jesus tells us that he would rather us be hot or cold (good or bad) than to be lukewarm (complacent). God can work with desires and emotions, no matter at what level, as long as they are in action, but he cannot work with energies that have become static or lukewarm (Revelation 3:14-16).

Moses may have been "hot-headed," but he wasn't lukewarm and so God was able to use him. To be complacent is to be self-satisfied or pleased with oneself. Here again is another sign of selfishness. If you are self-satisfied then you feel that you don't need God therefore God can't use you as He did Moses.

When we come to the realization that we may die at the pigpen or whatever dire situation we find ourselves in, we get to the point where we've had enough and can't take any more and our fear and anger will force us to make a decision, as did Moses, to kill our physical addiction (taskmaster) and flee to the desert or that arid wasteland of our consciousness. It is there we will find spiritual guidance.

The Egyptian taskmaster soiled the virgin princess or in other words, our physical and material desires have spoiled in us all that's holy and pure. We have to put an end to it. If we don't end the souls suffering, we will constantly be at odds with ourselves. Moses was born a Hebrew but was living as an Egyptian. The soul or spirit living within us will always cry out to God to be free.

Jesus said, "When you give rise to that which is within you, what you have will save you. If you do not give rise to it, what you do not have will destroy you." The Gospel of Thomas v.70

The Desert

Moses represents the Christ Consciousness that lays waiting inside of us. The similarities of Jesus and Moses are unmistakable. Moses comes to us from the water (spirit) in a basket or wooden cradle, Jesus from the waters of the Jordan. Moses enters into Egypt (Self) and is drawn out of self through Jesus, who the Bible records as coming out of Egypt.

And so was fulfilled what was said through the prophet: "Out of Egypt I called my son." Matthew 2:15 (Hosea 11:1).

They both were protected at birth. In its infancy the Christ Consciousness is protected, hidden in the sub-conscious until it is time to manifest or show itself.

Even though you may not feel spiritual or say that you believe in spiritual things your sub-conscious is being exposed to the laws of the spirit on a daily basis. Even though we may not admit or accept the fruits of the spirit; love, kindness, mercy, forgiveness, etc., they exist in all of our lives. They are all around us.

As the Christ Consciousness grows stronger in your subconsciousness it will eventually try to take over the conscious mind. What you do and say will start to feel abnormal. The growing spiritual consciousness will make you start to feel guilty about your actions and cause you to start questioning what you do and why you do it. You will start to feel out-of-place and alone and you will start to question your actions and see yourself differently. I hear it every day that people are confused, looking for answers and a purpose to their lives. The Christ Consciousness is working in all of us.

When your anger and emotions become overpowering you may start to lose it as did Moses and all that you are and all that you have become will be in jeopardy. You will eventually cross the line with yourself, and like Moses will need to get away for a while. Moses fled to the desert to escape Pharaoh. When Pharaoh heard the news of the murder, he tried to have Moses killed.

Pharaoh represents that part of our mind that wants to hold us back or to keep us enslaved. Our own mind will fight against us, and our conscious mind will try and kill any thoughts we have of making a change in our life. So, you may have to get away for a while just to gather your thoughts.

The desert represents another place of awakening. The desert can invite deep reflection on spiritual realities. It is during Moses' time in the desert that he saw and heard the burning bush. Two things are going to happen during this time. One, you are going to feel different about what is going on around you. You are going to feel uneasy around the people with whom you use to associate yourself. This could include even your immediate family, but you will be mostly offended by those who gossip, slander, are arrogant, boastful, senseless, and faithless. It is like when you stop smoking cigarettes. Even though you may have smoked for years once you quit for a while you don't like to be around them because you can't stand the smell. You look at these people and are offended by their behavior and they remind you that you too use to be like them.

At this time, I suggest you get away, flee to the desert. Even if it is just to the local library or park but you need to start spending some time alone. My desert was the mountains. I logged over 300 trail miles in the Smoky Mountain National Park during my desert period and just like Moses I saw the burning bush. Well not literally.

The second thing that is going to happen is you are going to find a purpose in life. The burning bush represents purpose. For Moses it was to go back to Egypt and free his people from captivity. For me my burning bush was to write a book. The time I have spent reading and studying has freed me from the world. I found that I don't need a mate; a particular profession; that I can live on less money, and I no longer was scared to be alone with myself. What I realized was that it was me, my Pharaoh-ego, who was holding me captive, and it was my Moses-ego that had the power to free me.

Mostly what I discovered during my desert period was that we are never truly alone. We may feel we are in a desert place, a place in our mind that seemingly lacks substance (understanding) and life, but in Truth desert places do not exist. God is ever present even though we may not feel His presence and although we may feel we are lacking in some way God's resources are always available to us.

In Spirit there is no such thing as lack. When we realize this then we make our desert places into an oasis.

Jesus said, "I am the light above everything. I am everything. Everything came forth from me, and everything reached me. Split wood, I am there. Lift up a rock, you will find me there. The Gospel of Thomas v.77a-77b

Whatever sacrifice it takes there is no greater feeling than to be free. Ask yourself, who is really free? The man behind bars who is free to think as he pleases or the man who is physically free but is a prisoner in his own mind.

Before you start writing your memoirs your main purpose right now is the same as Moses' –to free Israel. And who is Israel? The seeker, and who is that seeker? It is you. It is time to free yourself from yourself and reign free.

Jesus said, "The seeker should not stop until he finds. When he does find, he will be disturbed. After having been disturbed, he will be astonished. Then he will reign over everything." The Gospel of Thomas v.2

The last bit of selfishness that you are harboring now must be dealt with. Even though your Pharaoh-ego doesn't want to let you go and give up its control over you before you can move Godward you have to leave Pharaoh and Egypt behind. This also includes those who are a bad influence on your life. They must be given up. They need control over you so they can keep sucking the life out of you. They feed off your negative energy that's why they want to keep you down. They are like emotional vampires needing your negative life blood to stay alive. They have no life of their own and need to feed off the living to fill alive.

These people in your life are not positive they are completely negative, and it is negativity that they crave. The gossiper needs more gossip, the hater needs more hate, the faithless needs the unfaithful, the slanderer needs to slander and the deceitful needs deceit. Remember, in the spirit like attracts like even if the spirit is an evil one – this is a law.

Too much negativity will destroy us; it is what is destroying the world. The sad reality is that if you live in this type of environment too long you too become negative and even if you escape this bad environment, you are still negative, and it is negativity that you crave. Most people who are in this shape don't know what it means to be positive because they've never experienced it. Their whole life has been nothing but drama and when the drama stops, they don't feel alive, so they jump back into another bad relationship or go back to the people who were causing all the drama so they can feed their negative cravings.

When the drama stops, they feel lost and confused. They feel empty, and instead of filling that emptiness up with something positive, they, like the dog, return to their vomit or go back to that situation that was making them sick. I've seen it time and time again: the woman who goes back to her abusive and cheating husband, or the child who keeps going back to their sexual, physical, or mental abusive parents.

In the spirit world, like attracts like. If your thoughts are negative, you will attract negativity and be drawn to it. Change your thoughts and change your life. This is why the Truth of God is so uplifting. It's all positive. Love is positive and the Truth of God is love! We are not sinful, unrighteous, and filthy rags! We are gods and children of the Most High! Don't let anyone and I mean anyone tell you differently. I was asked to leave a church because I said these positive truths. Even in church there are those who want to keep you down so they can keep making money from your suffering.

If you keep carrying negative thoughts of your past in your head, they will continue to manifest themselves negatively in your life. Change these thoughts to positive and you will start attracting a better life. For some this is hard to do because they can't forgive and forget. Like the story of Lot's wife, they can't stop looking back.

Jesus replied, "No one who puts his hand to the plow and looks back is fit for service in the kingdom of God." Luke 9:62

I don't know if you've ever plowed a garden, but I can tell you it's hard to plow a straight row if you're looking behind you. It's just as hard knowing where you're going in life if you keep looking back to the past. No wonder you can't keep your life straight. Pun intended.

The past hurts as long as you keep remembering it. The time has come now for you to start remembering a better past. It is time to move from the negative into the positive. It's time for you to break free of the negative attractions in your life. If you keep moving forward only to drag the past with you then today is only yesterday and there is no tomorrow.

Only you know what your Pharaoh is, but I will guarantee you there is something there in your life that you have not dealt with, but whatever it is if you don't deal with it soon it will follow you into the wilderness where it may become a stumbling block to your progress. The Israelites wondered in the desert for 40 years when the Promised Land was only a couple of months travel. And those Israelites that kept complaining and stayed negative they never reached the Promised Land. Whatever is holding you to your past it's time to let it go even if it hurts.

By faith Moses, when he had grown up, refused to be known as the son of the Pharaoh's daughter. He chose to be mistreated (suffer) along with the people of God rather than to enjoy the pleasures of sin for a short time. He regarded disgrace (suffering) for the sake of Christ as of greater value than the treasures of Egypt because he was looking ahead to his reward. By faith he left Egypt not fearing the king's anger; he persevered because he saw him who is invisible. Hebrews 11:24-27

The Purpose

Exodus in the Bible is the flight of Moses and the Israelites from Egypt. We have established that Israel are the seekers of God and Moses is one of our Super Conscious Egos that gives us the strength to deliver us from the material world. The Moses-ego is more than courage it is a feeling of self-worth, that I deserve more than this and that there must be something better.

As Hebrews 11:25 says, we should rather suffer for the sake of Christ (Truth) which is of greater value than for the treasures of this world and keep looking Godward to our reward. It is self-esteem or how I like to call it "self-steam," that give us the energy to get moving, to take charge of our life, but the Moses-ego, as with all egos, can be dangerous if it gets too inflated.

Most of the characters (alternate egos) in the Bible had large egos. Abraham was strong minded, Joseph was egotistical, Isaac, Esau, and Jacob too had large egos, but this is what got them through the hardships and helped them overcome the world. It is ok to embrace your big ego if it is going to help you leave the material world behind. The world has a big ego, and it will take another one just as big to defeat it. But don't let it get out of control if your thoughts become selfish you will have to meet them again at the pigpen.

These alternate egos are important in the fact your personal ego has been bruised and battered or you may never have developed an ego at all. You may have been exposed to so much negativity all your life that you don't have any self-worth or self-importance. But for most of us it was that big fat ego that led us to the pigpen in the first place and it was our egotistical personality that needed to be humbled.

Moses was the father of a purposeful life something we all are struggling to find. Moses was not happy with the circumstances of his life and his people, and he sought to change it no matter the cost.

Moses was a man who stumbled in his speech, and this was probably a good thing because he relied on God to furnish his words. Moses loved his people, and he brought them out of bondage and delivered them into the hands of a waiting Father. Even though he was imperfect, in God he was made perfect. This was a man I could admire and wanted to be like for I was not perfect but wanted very much to be perfect. So, I left my negative thoughts and picked up the positive actions of Moses and went head-to-head with my Pharaoh.

Then the Lord said to Moses, "See, I have made you like God to Pharaoh, and your brother Aaron will be your prophet. You are to say everything I command you, and your brother Aaron is to tell Pharaoh to let the Israelites go out of his country. But I will harden Pharaoh's heart, and though I multiply my miraculous things and wonders in Egypt, he will not listen to you. Then I will lay my hand on Egypt and with mighty acts of judgment I will bring out my divisions, my people the Israelites. Exodus 7:1-4

Multiplication and Division is one of The Creation Steps. To divide is to conquer and God always multiplies before He divides. Before God takes something away, He will give you something beforehand. Something you don't need will be taken away and something you do need will be given.

This could be most anything: a job, a mate, a friend, money, advice, spiritual help, the list goes on and on. You will see this more and more down the road so when extra things come be ready something is fixing to leave. But most importantly don't refuse the help of others, they have been sent to you for a reason. Watch for the signs and take what is offered.

In the book of Revelation Jesus said to the Church of Philadelphia, that the one who overcomes the world he will make a pillar in the temple of God. Well, that temple is your body, and that pillar is God's strength and power. If you are going to move a house, you build supports to hold it up before you knock the foundation out from under it. God is not going to pull the rug out from under you without having someone there to keep you from falling on your face and making a fool out of yourself. The support you need will be there, identify it and lean on it. It may be a friend, a family member, a church group or whatever but it will be there for you.

God has promised, *"Never will I leave you; never will I forsake you."* Hebrews 13:15 (Deuteronomy 31:6)

God will not abandon you in this time of need. I know this how, because for me my way main purpose in life is to be my brother's keeper and that means being a pillar for their temple. I know there are many more out there like me that are there waiting and hoping for another opportunity to help a brother or sister on their spiritual journey. Don't deny these people their blessing. If they want to give you advice listen, if they want to give you money take it. They will know your need before you do.

When you finally attune your thoughts and mind to God you will know instinctively what one needs and will be prepared to give it because it is only through service to others that you can earn the respect of God.

(Jesus said), "The King will reply, 'I tell you the truth, whatever you did for the least of these brothers of mine, you did for me.'" Matthew 25:40

On my spiritual journey I had a pastor and good friend help see me through. He was there to support and guide me and I will always be indebted to him and his family for their service. So, don't worry that you are in this alone someone is there waiting to pray you through.

Midian

Midian (Heb.) – *rule; government; judgment; striving; contending; pleading; strife; contention.*

As Moses fled from Pharaoh he ran to the land of Midian where the Bible says he sat by a well. A Midian Priest named Reuel (or Jethro) had seven (perfection) daughters who came to the well (spirit) to gather water to fill the troughs (souls) of their father's flock. As they were trying to draw water some shepherds came along and drove the women away, but Moses got up and came to their rescue and watered their flocks.

This is a symbol of the Christ Consciousness at work. Reuel (Heb.) – *led of God; Shepard of God; friendship of God; companion of God*, is a thought of divine guidance and care. Also, it is a sense of mutual understanding, fellowship, and comradeship between man and God. The Christ Consciousness is saying we are friends, we are comrades, we have a mutual understanding, we are one.

(Jesus said), *"You are my friends if you do what I command. I no longer call you servants, because a servant does not know his master's business. Instead, I have called you friends, for everything I learned from my Father I made known to you."* John 15:15

The seven daughters of Reuel or Jethro represent to me the seven steps of perfection needed for us to continue on our journey. Although we try in life to be good and do what's right sometimes the steps Godward are difficult to follow.

There will always be those selfish individuals (shepherds) that will try and drive us away from the well of living waters – Spirit. It will happen in the mental and it will also happen in the physical or material. Selfishness will always exist around us, but the Moses-ego in us or the Christ Consciousness will come to our rescue and drive the selfish thoughts from our mind and in doing so will give birth to new thoughts and purpose.

After the rescue of the seven daughters Moses was invited to eat with Ruel and his family. Ruel, the priest, gave to Moses one of his daughters in marriage, Zipporah, and they had a son named Gershom which means *"I have become an alien in a foreign land"*.

As these new thoughts are conceived in our mind they are "alien" to us, but as we see with Moses when we are invited into to eat with the Master, we will start to feel that there is a place where we belong. A place far off but yet so near.

Zipporah (Heb.) – *little bird; sparrow; chirper; twitterer,* represents these new thoughts that are free as a bird. Although they are free thoughts, they still have their limitations but when married to our Moses-ego are being drawn forth in consciousness and led away from darkness of the subconsciousness that Egypt represents.

The disciples said to Jesus, "Tell us what the Kingdom of Heaven is like. He replied, "It is like a mustard seed, the smallest of all. However, when it falls into worked ground it sends out a large stem, and it becomes a shelter for the birds of Heaven. The Gospel of Thomas v.20

Birds signify, free, swift thoughts that unite heaven and earth. The Christ is our refuge and shelter for our most precious spiritual thoughts.

Median was the fourth son of Abraham (faith) by his second wife Keturah (*incense; perfume*). Keturah represents in us a phase of the soul-conscious that is still in the sense state but aspires to higher things for the body. Although our subconscious (soul) is still dominated by sense consciousness it is being inspired by the Super Conscious or Higher Self, and as we aspire for higher and purer realizations of Truth this inspiration begins in us a transmutation or the action of changing our sense state of consciousness into another form – Spiritual Consciousness or Christ Consciousness.

Our desire for higher truths prepares us for transmutation or the state of being changed into another form. The animal nature of Natural-man is being transformed into or should I say, back to, our godly nature – Spirit-man. Our sense thoughts may be the dominate consciousness, but it is in a state of strife and contention causing us pain and suffering. Our fear is losing power over us in preparation for our sense state of consciousness to be transformed into the higher spiritual consciousness. Fear is probably the biggest obstacle to overcome. Fear is the first sign of sin entering in or the first sign of missing the mark and falling short of perfection. Fear is part of the sense-consciousness and as this consciousness dissipates so too will fear vanish.

The Midianites

The Midianites were enemies of the Israelites. Israel represents the reality of spiritual ideas in consciousness which are opposed to those thoughts represented by the Midianites. The Midianites represent thoughts in sense consciousness that are likely to cause arguments, thoughts that are judgmental and thoughts that discriminate. These sense thoughts must be eliminated from consciousness thus the judgment.

Midianites, as part of our sense-consciousness brings contention and strife. We, like the Israelites have not fully accepted the spiritual consciousness and are not strong enough to hold steady and let the divine power do its perfect work within us. This will come later. Instead, we are holding on to false-ideas, false-thoughts and thought-errors associated with our sense-consciousness. The result is strife inside and outside of us. We project what we feel and feel what we project. Strife, petty quarrels, jealousies are hard for most people to eliminate from their lives because they keep creating them and thus have to keep meeting them.

This is why they never move Godward and why they keep hanging around at the pigpen. They will never eliminate strife from their life until they reach the higher spiritual consciousness – the Christ Consciousness or the mind that was in Jesus. Strife must be wholly and completely out of our life before we can possess the Promised Land.

At this degree of understanding we are zealous for our limited understanding of the Truth and do whatever it takes to defend these beliefs to the point of destroying anything that interferes with their freedom. The thought that seeks to destroy those who oppose us reacts, and we find our own people in contention. This leads to self-examination (judgment) and to the revelation that we have been in great error and tried to hide our sin in the deceptions of matter. This sin calls down on us the wrath of the moral law, and Truth is obscured from us for a time. But have no fear the all-possibility is about to manifest from another view-point – the well of living waters.

This new idea is being draw-out of us (Moses) which works from the inside out and if we will allow the progressive work of the Holy Spirit and apply this in our life, we will see good things start to manifest in our lives.

For the transformation to begin we must go away, flee to the desert, or go to the solitude within and lead our flock of religious thoughts to the back of the wilderness, where dwells the exalted One, the I AM, whose kingdom is good judgment and not how the world judges. The things we are discussing are not only things outside of us but are things within us. Moses, Pharaoh, Egypt, Israel etc., are all in the consciousness of man. The earth is the realm of experience where man's thoughts are projected outward so he can meet them and understand them.

Jesus said, "Recognize what is right in front of you, and that which is hidden from you will be revealed to you. Nothing hidden will fail to be displayed." The Gospel of Thomas v.5

If we don't visualize our thoughts, then they just swirl around in our head never to be eliminated.

The Burning Bush

One day while Moses was tending the flock of his father-in-law the priest of Median, he led his flock to the far side of the desert called Horeb (*desolation; desert; barren; solitude*). There the angel of the Lord appeared to Moses in flames of fire within a bush. Moses saw that although the bush was on fire it didn't burn up. So, Moses goes over to investigate and then God called to him from within the bush saying, "Moses!" "Moses!" which Moses responded, "Here I am."

The Lord told Moses not to come any closer and to remove his sandals because the place where he was standing was holy ground. Then God introduces Himself as the God of Abraham, Isaac, and Jacob. God tells Moses that He has heard the cry of the Israelites and seen their misery and was concerned about their welfare. God continues and tells Moses that He has come down to rescue them from the Egyptians. God tells Moses to go to Pharaoh and tell him to let God's people go and to bring them out of captivity.

Our time in the desert represents a place of awakening. It was during Moses' time in the desert that he experienced God firsthand at the burning bush. The burning bush appeared to Moses in a vision. This vision is the point where we are awakened to the true purpose for which we entered into the earth and realize the possibilities within that would aid us in fulfilling that purpose.

But like Moses, we are afraid that we can't achieve this task. That we are not strong enough to spiritualize our thoughts. We have been living in Egypt too long. God tells Moses not to worry that He would be with him and with a mighty hand compel the king of Egypt to release the Hebrews from slavery. This is where God is talking to you and letting you know that He has heard your cry and listened to your prayers and now is making Himself known to you.

The burning bush represents, in man, his spinal column - the nerve center through which our life energy flows. Like electricity running through a wire creating light, the energy within burns but doesn't consume. In mental activity, there is a vibratory process that uses up our nerve tissue, but in the wisdom that comes from God the nerve tissue is not consumed. Every day, our thoughts use up millions of brain cells, but fortunately, we produce millions of brain cells daily. But like the burning bush, our thoughts of God, and even our conversations about God, don't consume our brain cells. In fact, these conversations increase our brain's ability to function properly. This being true you would think more people would want to talk about God. It's been my experience that most people don't want to talk about God but would rather talk about the world, which is only burning more brain cells.

In the Bible, fire is commonly used as a symbol of destruction, especially when dealing with topics such as evil and error (sin).

Jesus said, "Whoever is near to me is near the fire. Whoever is far from me is far from the Kingdom. The Gospel of Thomas v.82

Fire represents the positive, affirmative state of mind as opposed to water which represents negation or the negative state of mind. Fire also stands for cleansing and purification. Fire in Truth is the fire of Spirit or the divine energy or life-giving force. This Spiritual fire never ceases in its life-giving and purifying qualities. In the regenerative man, it is constantly purifying his mind and thoughts until there is no error left to be consumed. After it has finished its cleansing work, it becomes in him an eternal flame or eternal life.

...for our "God is a consuming fire." Hebrews 12:29 (Deuteronomy 9:19)

By now on your journey, you are becoming more interested in God and spiritual things. Once you turn your attention to the inner fire that is burning in your heart and mind, God will start to reveal Himself as He did with Moses.

Like Moses you will realize that you are standing on holy ground. The outer consciousness, or sense-consciousness, can't handle this powerful energy; the current is too strong. This is why those who have not reached this step don't want to discuss these spiritual truths because it is too painful to talk about. The Truth is too powerful for them to grasp. All they want to do is end the conversation and get as far away from you as they can.

I once had this advanced conversation with someone who said they were a devout Christian and the longer we talked the madder they became, to the point they were ready to fight me. They told me to just 'walk-away,' which I immediately obliged, but not without pointing out their 'Christian-like' attitude.

This inner fire must be approached by pure spiritual thought, and until all our thought-errors are all consumed, the fire is too intense for us to endure. Like Jesus said, speaking as the Word of God, if you are next to me, you are next to the fire. Spiritual fire is life-giving; it does not destroy but purifies and renews. However, it will burn.

Moses Returns

After Moses and God finish their burning-bush conversation, Moses prepares to return to Egypt. He bids his father-in-law goodbye, puts his sons and his wife on a donkey and heads back to Egypt. God prepares Moses's brother Aaron for Moses' return, and they combine their efforts to free the Israelites. Remember I said that God multiplies before he divides.

Aaron (Heb.) – *illumined; enlighter,* was the first priest of Israel. Metaphysically Aaron's roll was as an intellectual light (*enlighter*) to the Israelites. The intellectual light is the ruling power or highly developed intellect. Intellect is the faculty of reasoning and objective understanding.

At this time, like Moses, you may have feelings of doubt and fear. Moses felt he would not be a good spokesperson because he stuttered. He felt he was unable to lead his people because they did not know him. But as he applied himself, he outgrew his limitations and gradually became aware of the "I AM" within.

I want you to understand something. Although you may feel as Moses felt that you are not capable of freeing yourself from your material bondage, God's Word will direct and guide you on your journey. Just keep self out of the way and let God speak or it may be that someone will speak for you. Aaron was well-spoken, so God made him Moses' spokesperson. God said to Moses,

"You shall speak to him and put words in his mouth; I will help both of you speak and will teach you what to do." Exodus 4:15

God will always have someone around to help you with your return. Someone will be your mouthpiece to announce to the world that God is working in you and through you. And later, as you will see, God will bring an aide to you as he brought Joshua to Moses to help you interpret these new signs and wonders.

Just be looking for them and recognize them when they come to you. They may come to you in the most unlikely places.

When you feel that you have found your purpose in the desert it is time to put into activity that purpose for which you have come into this earth plane; to undo that which has been done in error. You will start to see that what you once considered to be right was in fact incorrect. This is the point where you will start to meet yourself. By that I mean recognizing in others the sinful thoughts, deeds, and actions that they are doing is the same thoughts, deeds, and actions you had or are continuing to have. This is a period where we realize that we are reaping all the bad that we have sown in our life and now it is time to start sowing good so that the next harvest will be better.

Once we realize we have a purpose, or a "calling" we should not let fear or ignorance hold us back. And this ignorance and fear may apply to you or to others in your life. We can't take the attitude that because God has called me out that in God's eyes, I'm more special. In God's eyes we are all equal. No group or people or person is more superior than any other. God is not a respecter of persons. God does not show favoritism or partiality.

Then Peter began to speak: "I now realize how true it is that God does not show favoritism but accepts men from every nation who fear him and do what is right" Acts 10:34-35

With this newfound purpose we need to bring an attitude of universal brotherhood in which no race or special group is favored. Remember we are all God's children, and God is calling for us all to return home. Once we've identified our purpose, we must not be slow in our efforts to fulfill our purpose. We must be constantly busy, up working and doing that purpose for which we have been called. Don't put off tomorrow what needs to be done today. The time is now and as we pursue our purpose guidance will be given; direction will be shown, and further enlightenment will follow.

You may be assured that all our "try" will be counted as righteousness and although it may seem to others that we have no purpose, or our purpose is in vain, it is actually the contrary as long as we keep trying.

His disciples asked him: "When will you appear to us? When will you we see you?" Jesus replied, "When you strip naked without shame and trample your clothing (body) underfoot just as little children do, then you will look at the son of the living one without being afraid." The Gospel of Thomas v.37

When we bare our soul the divine will be revealed to the world and the light within us will be seen and that perfect light; that perfect love, will cast out all fear.

The Hardening of Hearts

Realization is step #8 of The Prodigal Steps. Remember the number 8 is a new beginning. Now that you have realized that it is time to accept God it is time to Reconcile, Reclothe and Rejoice (Steps 12, 13 & 14).

Again, I want to emphasize that although it appears that you are following a list of steps and as you finish one you move on to the next, but the steps are always there and exist in many forms. The steps are seen in the creation of things, in relationships, in the path to enlightenment, etc., they are constantly at work to help you meet yourself. This is why it is so valuable that you learn these steps and can identify them in any situation.

Just as the Ten Plagues that Moses brought against Egypt made a good story or movie, these plagues also apply to the individual. Remember you are Egypt, the body-consciousness. Just like the Egyptians and the Israelites for that matter, the power of the living God must be impressed upon your mind (Reclothe).

The following plagues may seem to you as the work of Satan but in actuality it is the power of God at work in you. As God did with Pharaoh, He may harden your heart and harden the hearts of others against you and just as the forefathers and even Jesus had to face the trial and temptation so will you. It will feel at this time that everything and everyone in the world is against you and you will feel that you are being attacked from all sides. But this period of Reconciliation is the time to restore your relationship with the Father.

Jesus said, "Blessed are you when they hate and persecute you. No place will be found where they persecuted you." The Gospel of Thomas v.68

The Pharaoh that was in power when Moses returned to Egypt was not the same Pharaoh that was in control when he fled to the desert. Remember Moses was raised in Pharaoh's house but not this Pharaoh.

This wasn't the same Pharaoh, so Moses wasn't remembered. For Pharaoh to allow the Israelites to leave Egypt the power of God had to be shown to the new Pharaoh and to the Egyptians. The Israelites too would get their first look at the power of the living God. The miracles that Moses and Aaron were about to perform were not merely magic tricks but actual manifestations of God's supernatural power.

The Egyptians had their own magicians who were skilled in the art of manipulation of three-dimensional laws. Through the ability of materialization and mind control they could make sticks turn into snakes or have grains of sand change into lice or fleas. Yet Moses and Aaron were able to go beyond these simple parlor tricks because they were attuned to an infinite source of Creative Energy.

During this time in your preparation to leave Egypt behind others will try to change your mind. Even your own mind will try to convince you to return to your old ways. You may even feel that your mind is playing tricks on you. People will try through thought-control and manipulation to make you see things differently. They will tell you that what you are feeling and seeing is nothing more than you losing your mind. Don't listen to them.

If the people believed Moses was merely a better magician than the Egyptians, they never would have wanted to leave Egypt and freed from their captors. As with the Hebrews, you must believe that God is speaking through your Moses-ego, and that your Moses-ego is manifesting His power. You must believe that God is in control and is more powerful than any physical or material force. Moses tried to tell his people that all the magic could be theirs if they would attune themselves to God and use it for His purpose. That same power can be yours if you will only believe.

Human nature does not change. We say we believe in God, but every time a hardship or difficulty arises, we falter in our beliefs. The same parlor tricks that were used in Moses' day are the same tricks being used today. We just call them by different names. Scientists today are not only working with three-dimensional law; they are using God's laws in other ways. Their discoveries may be used for the glorification of the Spirit on earth, or they may be used in the destruction of everything that is good, including the best that is within us.

Unless our Pharaoh-ego, and all those around us who oppose God's works, have their hearts 'hardened' (unfeeling), there can never be a great desire in us to follow our Moses-ego. All the plagues to come are necessary to raise morale and consciousness of the individual who has been enslaved by their own selfishness. That includes you as well.

Moses returned to Egypt with a higher state of consciousness which came from his time in the desert. Now the knowledge he obtained demanded application. Scripture tells us that knowledge not applied is sin. Moses had foreknowledge of the slaying of the first-born (physical) and knew he had to prophesy this to Pharaoh if Pharaoh refused to release the Hebrews. Moses certainly believed in the divinity of his mission, and the fact that God's protection, for what he was called to do, was almost certain death under the laws of the state.

If you don't break the addiction, if you don't conquer the Pharaoh-ego, if the soul is not set-free then under the law of God death physically and spiritually is certain.

Jesus said, "Wretched is a body depending on a body, and wretched is a soul depending on these two." The Gospel of Thomas v.87

The Plagues

As the awakening comes and as you start to attune yourself to God's Will and purpose, a higher consciousness, the Spiritual

Consciousness begins to emerge. This spiritual consciousness cannot be suppressed by the physical consciousness.

The people around you who are not attuned to the spirit are compelled to see things as physical only, they cannot see the spiritual or as Jesus put it, they cannot see the Kingdom. They are looking for things revealed physically and cannot see the spiritual side of the world. Only when you attune yourself to God will you start to see the Kingdom.

They said to him, "Tell us who you are so that we can believe in you. He replied: "You analyze the appearance of the sky and the earth, but you don't recognize what is right in front of you, and you don't know the nature of the present time." The Gospel of Thomas v.91

First you must learn to govern yourself. You must learn patience, mercy, kindness, judgment and understanding, and as you apply this "new" understanding in your life and don't abuse it, you will find the ability to bring harmony, peace, and understanding in every experience of your life, physically and socially.

The judgments of God on Egypt were called plagues. Each of these plagues has a special meaning to the physical and spirit – mind, body, and soul. We might say the 10 plagues are symbolic of the various stages of the evolution of the consciousness.

<u>Plague 1.</u>   <u>The Nile (water) turned to blood.</u> (Exodus 7:17-24)

It has been said that physical evolution emanates first from water. Water represents the spirit, and the blood represents that spirit in the physical. This is what is called the "first-born" or that of self-awareness. Redemption, or the action of being saved from sin (error), comes through the shedding of blood, or the sacrificing of self for the ideal. This pattern was shown to us by Jesus. Individually, we all have our own shedding of blood to do. Not physically as Jesus did, but in giving up our self-will for God's Will.

Symbolically, the "first-born" of any situation, from Cain (selfishness) on down, seems to represent the selfish impulses that brought about our involvements in materiality. What is the first reaction in any situation – SELF. To shed blood is to separate the spiritual from the physical or self from our selfishness.

Is it God's Will be done or is it my will be done? Scripture tells us that there is no remission of sin save through the shedding of blood. It is only through tribulation and sacrifice that we shed selfishness from our activities.

In fact, the law requires that nearly everything be cleansed with blood, and without blood, and without the shedding of blood there is no forgiveness. Hebrews 9:22

In the ritual and tradition of sacrifice, blood stood for death, and depending on the context, it might stand for judgment, sacrifice, substitution, or redemption. This first plague should make you realize, or will make you realize, that something has to be sacrificed or given up. And what is to be sacrificed? The ego and self-will.

The red blood of flesh does not carry the power to cleanse our consciousness from the dead works it is only through the inpouring of Spirit or the Word of God into our life blood that we are cleansed.

Blood represents life and is the vehicle that carries life through the body, but it is not life itself. Blood is used to express a spiritual principle that rests upon pure ideals, yet it manifests in mind and body in concrete form when rightly used. When blood is rightly appropriated in the Word of God it can be used for the purification of the mind and the healing of the body. This is where we get that the "Blood of Christ" cleanses us of all sin.

In him we have redemption through his blood, the forgiveness of sins, in accordance with the riches of God's grace that he lavished on us with all wisdom and understanding. And he made known to us the mystery of his will according to his good pleasure, which he purposed in Christ, to be put into effect when the times will have reached their fulfillment – to bring all things in heaven and on earth together under one head, even Christ. Ephesians 1:7-10

Christ is the life blood of the Word of God. The Word, the Christ is a form of energy that transcends anything in which blood exists. Sins are not forgiven because Jesus shed his blood, that is the physical act. Sin is forgiven because the life blood, the Christ is poured into our conscious not poured out. The Bible says that those who believe in Christ will not perish. It is those who except the Truth and feel sure of the Truth of God's Word that will live for eternity because the Spirit gives life it does not take it away.

<u>Plague 2.</u>   <u>The Visitation of Frogs</u> (Exodus 8:1-5)

The Egyptians raised frogs for food and considered them a great delicacy. The visitation of frogs showed the Egyptians that the Hebrews God had the power to raise instantly something that took the Egyptians great care and time to produce. During this period don't be afraid to let go of all the things that may have taken a lifetime to accumulate. The job, the spouse, the home etc., things you've worked so hard and so long for. As in the story of Job all this can be taken away in only a moment, and only a moment for God to restore it.

When all these blessings and curses I have set before you come upon you and you take them to heart wherever the Lord your God disperses you among the nations, and when you and your children return to the Lord your God and obey him with all your heart and with all your soul according to everything I command you today, then the Lord your God will restore your fortunes and have compassion on you and gather you again from all the nations where he scattered you. Deuteronomy 30:1-3

Until you are willing to rid yourself of your obsession to own and possess material things you will never know the spiritual things that are in store for you. As I stated before I lost just about everything that I had obtained in my life but eventually all these things were restored.

<u>Plague 3.</u>   <u>The Infestation of Gnats</u> (Exodus 8:16-19)

Gnats demonstrates God's power to create living creatures such as insects, from an unnatural source. It could be said that the lice were the natural result of the water having been turned to blood. The very moisture in the ground, if it were blood instead of water, would have made a natural breeding ground for these blood sucking insects.

The physical afflictions brought on by the curse of the lice could be seen as less a supernatural thing and more of a natural occurrence. Everyone at times gets sick. The plague of lice has more of a mental or emotional attachment. Lice can be anything physically that sucks the life blood or energy out of you.

The plagues are trials and tribulation that are brought upon you "for the shedding of blood" but the lice curse will probably come as a physical attack for the first three plagues deal with the physical. So don't be afraid if you physically get sick. At first your possessions and livelihood are attacked and then you are personally attacked. This may not seem fair because these plagues were brought by God on the Hebrews enemies but as you will see the Israelites were also affected by the first three plagues.

<u>Plague 4.</u>   <u>Flies and the Favor of Divine Influence</u> (Exodus 8:20-32)

In the fourth plague we find the first difference in the Egyptians' feelings toward the children of Israel.

The flies that were swarming the Egyptians were not swarming the Israelites. The Egyptians were beginning to realize that the Hebrews were favored by a divine influence.

Pharaoh was willing to permit the children of Israel to rest from their labors a few days and make sacrifices to their god, but Moses could not accept this. He knew he had to get the people out of the land entirely and away from the Egyptian influence.

As the awareness of the spiritual consciousness grows you will see and feel how different you are from most of the world or at least your personal world. This is a transition point from the physical to the mental. You will feel the need to end the physical cravings because you are now aware that if you don't get entirely away from them you will be right back to where you started. You will notice that the physical is still being attacked but the mental is not being affected. Although the physical needs are still there the mental need or cravings are starting to diminish.

However, if you don't flee from your Egypt (physical or material bondage) and get away from your Pharaoh-ego you will again be enslaved by the physical cravings. You can't take a rest period or a sabbatical year off to sort things out, you've got to leave, and leave now! Although Pharaoh may be willing to give you some time off once this time has ended its back to the salt mines.

At this point you will start to see that the people around you are affected more by your change than it is affecting you. This is the beginning of their hardening their hearts against you but it's the only way to break free.

<u>Plague 5.</u>   <u>Disease of Cattle and other Beasts of Burden</u>
(Exodus 9:1-7)

As the awareness of the spiritual consciousness continues the thought of the physical has now turned to the mental. This is The Prodigal Steps as the first seven steps pertain to the body and the second steps of seven have to do with the mind. Are you starting to see how these steps keep recurring? They will until you reach the Christ Consciousness.

With a new live comes new feelings of worry and doubt. How is this new life going to affect me personally and physically? What is it going to cost me professionally and financially? The fifth plague was striking at the Egyptian's source of revenue and food supply. The disease on the cattle and the other beasts of burden was costing them money.

After the third plague the children of Israel were not afflicted it was just the Egyptians who were affected. The Israelites seemed to be immune after the fifth plague. Perhaps they were becoming more in tune with Moses' purpose and such things did not come near them. With the proper attitude you will not be disturbed by the worries of your personal or professional life.

By now you are seeing the higher power at work, and you are getting excited about your newfound purpose, and you are ready to follow that purpose no matter where it may take you.

As for me at this point my health took a turn for the worse. I was sick and I knew it. My doctor said that if I didn't start several medications that I could die. Also, at this time I lost my job and the girl I was intending to marry. But these losses didn't affect me mentally. I saw it coming. Knowing and understanding the steps gave me foresight of what was to come, whether I liked it or not.

I had a long conversation with myself and God and swore to God if He did not reveal to me the Truth that I was seeking that I was ready to blow hell wide open. I also promised God that if He showed me His promises were true that I would never again question His authority. Six months later I went back to the doctor and all my vitals were back to normal. I eventually found another job, and it was probably a blessing that I didn't get married. So don't worry, be patient. I can testify that all of God's promises are true, but they are on God's schedule, not ours.

<u>Plague 6.</u> <u>Boils</u> (Exodus 9:8-12)

Boils are usually caused by a blood condition. The Egyptians blood had become susceptible to boils because of conditions resulting from the previous plagues. However, the children of Israel were immune. The Israelites may have received guidance from Moses on how to keep their blood purified.

When we are sincere in our efforts, the next step will be shown to us, but one step must be completed before we take the next. As you continue the process to ridding yourself of physical bondage, a period of purification will begin. There will be more craving for spiritual things than for physical things, but the physical will continue to try and overtake the spiritual. The boils are an indication of what is going on inside of the body. The spiritual and the physical will be warring with each other for dominance. If you've been emotional up to this point, then you haven't seen anything yet. The shedding of blood is not an easy process, so be advised a storm is approaching.

<u>Plague 7.</u> <u>Hailstorm</u> (Exodus 9:13-35)

Therefore, at this time tomorrow I will send the worst hailstorm that has ever fallen on Egypt, from the day it was founded till now. Exodus 9:18

Can't say that I didn't warn you. This may be the hardest battle you have ever fought or will fight in your life. The physical is not going to go down without a fight. This is going to affect you physically, emotionally, materially, and mentally and it is going to be a tough decision to make whether you want to fight or fold.

The plague of the hailstorm was the first plague in which the choice of the individual became the governing factor. With the forewarning of the hail, every individual had the opportunity to choose whether to believe in the power of God and Moses, or trust in Pharaoh's protection. Are you ready to trust in God, or do you want to keep relying on self or ego for answers?

This is the first time Pharaoh repented and admitted that he and his people were wicked. Human nature has not changed much from that day to this. As soon as things returned to normal, Pharaoh returned to his old ways. So be careful that you don't make this same horrible mistake. This may be the first time that you cried out to God for relief. Cry, shout, scream whatever it takes just know it will soon pass.

For his anger lasts only a moment, but his favor lasts a lifetime; weeping may remain for a night, but rejoicing comes in the morning. Psalm 30:5

<u>Plague 8.</u>   <u>Locusts</u> (Exodus 10:1-20)

After the hailstorm, the Egyptian people knew they had better heed the warning about the locust. Locust feed on the harvest. They are destroyers of the crops of the field. All that we have previously sown may be destroyed by these symbolical creatures. If we have nothing, we have nothing to go back to.

The Egyptians wanted Pharaoh to let Moses and his people go. They pleaded with Pharaoh, but he would not concede. He had been taught from his birth that he was an all-powerful god. It must have been difficult for him to acknowledge that the Israelite's God was superior.

Some people who start this process can't go through with it. The bonds of the past life are just too strong. They're afraid to give their life up completely to God. For those who choose to go forward, the people you love and care for may not be ready to accept the change they see in you. The friends and family that you have built in your life are not ready for the change. Their hearts will remain hardened toward you. They may say that they will go along with this madness but in truth they don't understand it therefore they will not accept it.

This is why God is Jehovah, he is a personal God.

This may be the last time you have a choice over your life. Give up now is to give in to defeat. To give up now and try to return to your old life will be a disaster. Most of what you previously had in your life is gone. To give up now everyone will see you as the failure that they always said you were. They will have won, and you will have lost. They again are your master, and you again are their slave. So today, right now, is the time to choose who you are going to serve.

<u>Plague 9.</u>   <u>Darkness</u> (Exodus 10:21-28)

Moses would not accept Pharaoh's conditions. When Pharaoh, in his wrath, told Moses not to try and see him again, Moses said, "Thou has spoken well." After that Moses dealt directly with the people.

The time will come when those on whom you have trusted will turn against you. They will not want to have further dealings with you and will turn their back on you. This is best, for it is time to start dealing directly with yourself.

The plague of Darkness signifies the spiritual darkness (Ignorance) of an individual who continually refuses to recognize or use the light (Knowledge and wisdom) that is offered.

"This is the verdict: Light has come into the world, but man loved the darkness instead of light because their deeds were evil. Everyone who does evil hates the light and will not come into the light for fear that his deeds will be exposed. But whoever lives by the truth comes into the light, so that it may be seen plainly that what he has done has been through God". John 3:19-21

It's time to step out of the darkness and into the light.

Plague 10.	Consecration of the First-Born (Exodus 12:29-30)

Before the last plague, Moses prepared his people for their departure from Egypt. He knew the tenth plague would be the final one.

The Israelites were to cleanse their bodies by eating certain specially prepared foods and their doors were to be marked with the blood of the sacrifice. This act gave the people a chance to express and show their allegiance to God.

"Passing over" is symbolic of moving from the physical-consciousness to the mental-consciousness or subconscious. Everything from this point on that the Israelites (the seekers) did would have a symbolic or underlying meaning attached. The marked door with the blood of sacrifice is symbolically saying that on one side of the door is physical death (smiting the first-born) and on the other side is eternal life. The only way we can enter that door is '*under the blood*' or sacrificing the flesh (self). Through the cleansing of our minds and aligning our thoughts, purpose, and our will with God's Will, we will escape the death angel – the second death.

Consecrate means to make or declare sacred. It is the action of declaring bread and wine (the elements of the Eucharist) to be or represent the body and blood of Christ Jesus. It is also to dedicate to some service or goal. We must give our first-born to God. We must give our life over to His purpose and when we do this we will pass under the physical-blood as we enter the spiritual-door to eternal life.

In the days to come the Israelites were to remember what the Lord had done for them. *"With a mighty hand"* the Lord had rescued them from their captors.

In the days to come, when your son asks you, "What does this mean?" say to him, "With a mighty hand the Lord brought us out of Egypt, out of the land of slavery. When Pharaoh stubbornly refused to let us go, the Lord killed every first-born in Egypt, both man and animal. This is why I sacrifice to the Lord the first male offspring of every womb and redeem each of my firstborn sons. And it will be like a sign on your hand and a symbol on your forehead that the Lord brought us out of Egypt with his mighty hand." Exodus 13:14-16

From this point on, you are to give your firstborn thoughts as an offering to God. Remember what was previously discussed. Our thoughts are our children, and our firstborn thoughts are usually from our self-will. Again, remember it was your self-willed thoughts that led to the pigpen. The firstborn thoughts are selfish and must be sacrificed. These thoughts must be given up to God so that the next thoughts will be from God so His Will is done. This is hard for most people because we love to put our two cents in.

Earthly advice is just that, of the Earth and for the Earth but it is not our earthly advice that counts most; most of it is just useless information and trivia. All that really matters is what is eternal and that is, the Truth. Remember what Paul said, '*first the natural man then the spiritual man.*' Our first thoughts that we speak are always based on our feelings, emotions, and personal opinions. This is the sense-consciousness talking, not the Christ Consciousness.

I find it ironic that the Day of Atonement (the reconciliation of God and man brought about by the life and death of Christ) falls on October 10, the tenth day of the tenth month. The Prodigal Steps, number ten is "Repent." Repent is to have a change of heart and mind that brings us closer to God. We must repent before we are Reconciled (step #12).

I also find it ironic that we are also to give a tenth of our firstborn earnings as an offering to God. Ten is also the number representing Journey or Wilderness or the place where these practices were instituted and where we are to follow the Israelites example.

After the death of the firstborn, the Egyptians were glad to lend the Israelites anything they had, just to be free of them. God had promised Moses that they would not leave empty-handed. Even when He told Moses to leave, Pharaoh asked for Moses' blessing. Evidently Pharaoh now feared Moses and was in awe of his power, or perhaps he wanted assurance Moses would not continue to call curses on him. Then the Egyptian people, too, almost demanded that Pharaoh humble himself before Moses. This shows the power a people may exert, even under a mighty ruler.

If enough pressure is applied, the people can demand their rights. The Egyptians were afraid that if Pharaoh did not agree to Moses' demands they might all die. The people had suffered because of their ruler's selfishness and were more affected by the first nine plagues than Pharaoh and his family. For this reason, the people were forced to work harder to keep Pharaoh supplied with all the things which he and his family were accustomed to having. Let this be a lesson to all of us. The selfishness of our leaders will have a lasting impact on our lives. Their errors are our sufferings. The tenth plague, which took Pharaoh's first-born son, touched him for the first time.

If your Pharaoh-ego continues to be stubborn and does not free your soul, then the physical body will demand it. If you don't free the soul, it will bring death to what's left of you. Because of your ego those around you, have suffered including your own body. The plagues will come to bring humbleness and death to the ego. Once free from the Pharaoh-ego you will be able to leave the fleshpots of Egypt behind. But you will not leave empty handed, that energy you have been using to feed your ego will now be used to build spiritually and you are going to need all your spiritual energy to make it through the wilderness.

Because we have the gift of free-will there is nothing but the nature of our own desires that binds us to any condition. If we listen to that still voice inside of us instead of our own selfishness, then we can leave our "Egypt" anytime. Once our desires are in relation to the laws of Creative Force we will experience life to its fullness. If we care only for those experiences that satisfy or gratify self without the thought of how they will affect our life as well as the life of others, then our disobedience will be a stumbling block to our journey Godward.

STEP 11

Transition | Disorder

Transition – *The process or a period of changing from one state or condition to another.*

Disorder – *A state of confusion.*

Mental Unfoldment

The Pharaoh-ego, until weakened and humbled by the "shedding of blood", will keep our spiritual energy represented by the Israelites, suppressed, using it for the ego's own desires. Once we release this energy, and are willing to follow it, the I AM within us will lead us Godward and back to at-onement with the Creative Forces. With the use of the Creative Forces, we will reach the Promised Land and the new state of consciousness. The crossing of the Red Sea is another emblem, or symbolic expression of the move into the new state of consciousness – The Christ Consciousness.

The Bible, from Abraham to Christ, is a pattern of mental unfoldment. All that manifests in the material world is a shadow of that mental or spiritual import. To be at-one with the Creative Force depends on how we apply the Creative Force and for what purpose. If the Creative Force is only used to manifest our selfish desires, then it will bring dis-ease and destruction. If our desire and purpose is selfless and used for service to others, then the Creative Force will bring health and harmony.

The pattern of mental unfoldment is developed through the willingness to be used for the service of others. When it is our constant desire to seek the Truth, and desire to do only the Will of the Father then the Creative Force will overpower our selfish desires and overcome our material appetite and overcome our earthly ego, but the first step toward "freedom" leads into the wilderness.

Mentally, once we decide to leave behind the material world and the sense-conscious, we must confront the subconscious, the repressed and hidden area of our mind. It is in our subconscious or our soul-mind that is stored our false-realities, our thought-errors and false beliefs that we have accumulated over our many lifetimes. Mind is the factor that is in direct opposition to the Will. Like the complaining children of Israel, our old habits, our conditioned thinking, our familiar and unquestioned attitudes, and responses, will scream out with desire to return to our old ways. Any step forward involves taking on new responsibilities, new obligations. This is hard for most because they would rather be bound in servitude than freed from responsibilities.

Until we bring under control our thought-errors that are in variance to the spiritual truths we will never be ready to cross the Jordan River into the Promised Land where there are more spiritual battles to be fought. When we have the courage to take the responsibility for the whole body –spiritual, mental, and physical –raising it from servitude to service, we are ready to enter the land of milk and honey. This is the purpose of The Wilderness Steps to further rid you of any selfishness; to make the body-mind and the soul-mind one with the spirit-mind and prepare you for the second coming of the Christ Consciousness. We were first created in the likeness and image of God. That is the first Christ. In the beginning it was created in us, the I AM, but we chose to leave it and chose self-will over God's Will. Now we have a chance to possess it again.

All must pass under the rod. As Moses and the children of Israel passed through the Red Sea they were baptized in the cloud and in the sea as an example of a physical separation from what they had built for themselves during their time in Egypt.

The physical body is the shell or temple that may be touched with hands. We must be born again so that we may dwell in those mansions not made with hands –but are prepared for those that have washed their robes, their bodies, their souls in the blood (the physical and the spiritual).

Jesus said, "I will give you that which eyes have not seen, ears have not heard, hand did not touch, and minds have not conceived." The Gospel of Thomas v.17

For us to know the Truth we must clearly understand the knowledge we gain through our own experiences and meditation with God. We must be born again in flesh and in spirit for our soul to clearly understand these same experiences.

We must awaken from the dream of mortality, leave Egypt (the flesh consciousness) forever, cross the Red Sea, the boundary line where we sacrifice every tie that binds us to the past; go through the wilderness (a transitory state); through the waters of the Jordan, the boundary line between the transitory state and the permanent state and plant our feet on Canaan's land – our inheritance.

The Red Sea

The Red Sea is a long, narrow sea that lies between Asia and Africa (Joshua 24:6). It is called the "sea" in most places in the Bible where it is mentioned. It was through this sea that the Israelites passed on dry land, while the Egyptians who followed them were drowned (Exod. 14:2-28).

Since his beginning in the earth plane man has believed he is separate from God. This fixed sea of universal thought-error has become part of the very world in which we live. These fixed thoughts or thought-errors have found their place in the sense-consciousness of mankind and become a part of his physical existence. Metaphysically the sea signifies universal mind of which we are all a part. It is a state of unrest; a sea of controversy; a sea of emotion, etc., it is the universal mind or that great realm of unexpressed and unformed thoughts that contains all potentiality; a sea of possibilities. In the book of Revelation, the beast with seven heads and ten horns comes out of the sea (Revelation 13:1). It is this sea or sea of universal sense thoughts that is cast into the bottomless pit of nothingness and is no more.

Then I saw a new heaven and new earth, for the first heaven and the first earth had passed away, and there was no longer any sea. Revelation 21:1

There is a universal life force, which moves upon a universal substance (understanding). This combination of life and substance is the matrix in which all mind force works; symbolically it is the Red Sea or life sea. Human thoughts, which form part of the race consciousness, have impregnated this sea with the ideas that the body is mortal and must be given up.

The Red Sea represents the sum of all the thoughts about life. In the mythology of the Greeks and Romans this is symbolized by the River Styx, over which the souls of the dead were ferried to the underworld by the ferryman Charon or Kharon. This river separated the worlds of the living and the dead. Metaphysicians view the sea as the psychic realm or race thought, which has to be overcome by the progressive soul.

The pattern of our mental unfoldment and our becoming at-one with the Creative Force is determined by our willingness to be used as a channel for the Creative Force that is to be manifested in the material world. We must move from servitude to service, to make our desires at-one with God's desires.

There is nothing wrong with having desires if they are in keeping with the Will of God. The constant desire to be at-one with the Creative Force will lead us out of the thrall of the appetites, the senses, or our ego.

The Unclean Spirit

Psychologically, once we decide to leave our world of a habitual consciousness, we must confront the subconscious (soul-mind), the repressed and hidden areas of our mind. If we can't come to God on our own the soul will cry out to God for redemption. Subconsciously we will start to feel that we need to change; that something is not right in our mind that we can't explain. But when we decide to make a change and leave our Egypt (physical desires) behind we have only temporarily dealt with the problem.

"When an evil [unclean) spirit comes out of a man, it goes through the arid places (mental desert the place between the conscious and subconscious mind) *seeking rest and does not find it. Then it says, 'I will return to the house* (body) *I left. When it arrives, it finds the house swept clean and put in order. Then it goes and takes seven other spirits more wicked than itself, and they go in and live there. And the final condition of that man is worse than the first."* Luke 11:24-26

If we don't start to fill up the emptiness of our subconscious mind with something more spiritual, then the old habits will come back to us and this time the urges will be seven times stronger. This is the biggest mistake that most people make when they begin to seek God. They believe that as soon as they have been saved and baptized that everything will be better. But in fact, they find that things continue to get worse, and they will get even worse if they don't start their wilderness journey soon. We can't sit still and wait for everything to fall into place we need to keep moving Godward. Most Christians are happy just to wait for the day that they believe they will be raptured away. That's just being selfish!

If we don't deal with our physical desires now, later they will destroy us. If we don't get a handle on our old bad habits, our unquestioned attitudes and responses, and our preconditioned thinking then we will always be tied to our past. If we don't experience our wilderness period we cannot cross the Jordan into the Promised Land, where there are more battles to be fought. Until we bring under control the conflicting aspects of SELF to a more spiritual function with the Will of God, then we will never have the courage to take on the responsibility for the Whole-Body.

Mind, Body and Soul

To truly be at-one with the Creative Force we must make the mind, body, and soul as one. At first, we were spirit or a heavenly body and then we entered our earthly body, now we need to make them both into one and the only way to do this is through the mind, for the mind is the builder. We in fact have many minds. Jesus said in my father's house are many abiding places or many levels of consciousness (John 14:2-6).

To make the body, mind, and spirit to function as one we must make their will to be the Will of the Creator. The will of the body, the will of the mind, and the will of the spirit must become as one. Just as the following commandment given by Christ Jesus, we must love God our Father with all our mind, body and soul and we must love our neighbor as we love our self as well. When we make the will of the three the Will of the Father then we have fulfilled this commandment. If not our body, mind and soul will always be in opposition to one another.

Jesus said, for there will be five in one house. Three will oppose two. Two will oppose three. The father will oppose his son and the son will oppose his father. And they will stand up and they will be alone. The Gospel of Thomas v.16b

God's Will and purpose will always be at odds with our physical mind, body, and soul. The three will always be in opposition with the two. We, as children, will always oppose our heavenly Father. If we stand against God and do not change our will to His Will then we will always be alone.

Jesus said, "Where there are three Gods, they are Gods. Where there are two or one, I am with him". The Gospel of Thomas v.30

When we understand that the three Gods – Father, Son, and Holy Spirit, are all one, functioning separately yet as one, then we can understand that this is also true for us, that our mind, body and soul are separate yet functioning as one. Then and only then, when we make our mind, body and soul function as one can we become at-one with three Gods, and this can only be achieved through the Christ Consciousness.

Jesus answered, "I am the way and the truth and the life. No one comes to the Father except through me [if you really have known me]. If you knew me, you would know my Father as well. From now on, you do know him and have seen him." John 14:6-7

Reuniting

In the flight from Egypt, the 600,000 men, with their families, household goods, and livestock, and all the things they 'borrowed' from the Egyptians, must have extended over a large area. In the wilderness of Zin, they were able to group together as a congregation for the first time.

This may be the first time that you are able to meet with others who are also in their wilderness journey. It will be a new and probably terrifying experience at first because you don't know where you are, you're not sure where you're heading and the only thing you are sure of is where you've been.

The Israelites having such a large number may not have ever heard Moses speak. His pronouncements were probably relayed by other people, increasing the chances of misinterpretations and distortions of his original messages. During this time in the wilderness some of those who are not so close to the word or have been misinformed or misinterpret the message start turning again to their SELF. At this point don't get in a hurry or get frustrated with those or the circumstances around you. Turning back at this point will only bring destructive forces against you, remember the eight evil spirits.

Shortly after the congregation assembled, the winds of rebellion (selfishness) began to blow and the whole congregation of the children of Israel began to murmur against Moses and Aaron.

In the desert the whole community grumbled against Moses and Aaron. The Israelites said to them, "If only we had died by the Lord's hand in Egypt! There we sat around pots of meat and ate all the food we wanted, but you have brought us out into this desert to starve this entire assembly to death." Exodus 16:2-3

At this point I hope you're not saying the same thing about me. That I have brought you this far for you to only suffer more. Remember you are in a period of transition. You haven't yet made it from the temporary consciousness to the permanent consciousness. I promise you the land of milk and honey is waiting for you.

Once the Israelites entered the desert it was only about an eleven-day travel to the Jordan River, but it took them 40 years to reach it. And the reason it took so long was that they were not ready to enter the Promised Land. The Israelites felt that God could help them, but they didn't believe they could take the land once they got there. As a result, they wandered in the desert for 40 years, until almost an entire generation of men and women died.

Until the last remaining amount of selfishness is purged from your mind, you, like the Israelites, will wander aimlessly in the wilderness. However long this may take, is up to you. The

Israelites wandered around for 40 years. I think my wandering was more like 42 years. It took me much longer. I just kept going around and around that mountain repeating the same old errors over and over again. Leaving my bad habits only to return to them again and again. This is the purpose of my book to help you make the transition quicker, so you don't wander around aimlessly for the rest of your miserable life.

The Real Enemy

Two months after the experience in the Red Sea, the real enemy of the Hebrews emerged. (Exodus 16:3). Until now, the oppressor had been external, the Egyptian oppressors, but now the one that lurked within began to emerge. This enemy was much more deadly than their former oppressors, who fed and clothed them.

The attitude and behavior of the Israelites against Moses and Aaron could have kept them embroiled in turmoil and forever wandering through the wilderness. The people were difficult, conflicting, and argumentative. However, it was their murmuring that most disturbed God.

The American Heritage Dictionary translates "murmur" as: *1. A low, indistinct, and continuous sound. 2. A grumbled complaint.* Murmuring is outwardly appearing to be content with the circumstance but under your breath continuously complaining.

It was your decision to make a change in your life, and you have started the process, but underneath it all, you may be unhappy with your decision. For those who are willing to continue this path, more will be added, but for those who start to complain, more will be taken away. Removing more and more of the world from you is the only way to show you the power of God, for the less you depend on the world for food and clothing, the more you will have to depend on God for those needs.

(Jesus said), "Therefore, I tell you, do not worry about your life, what you will eat or drink; or about your body, what you will wear. Is not life more important than food, and the body more important than clothes?" Matthew 6:25

When we worry, we start to murmur. Fear is the beginning of sin because when we think God is not going to provide for us, we take it upon our SELF to satisfy those needs. Complaining is just going to slow you down especially when you complain to others. They will remind you that they told you that following these steps was crazy. They won't hesitate to tell you that you were wrong, and they were right.

The Bittersweet Waters

As the Israelites left the Red Sea, they traveled three days into the desert without finding water. When they came to Marah (bitter) they could not drink the water because it was bitter. So, the people grumbled against Moses saying, "What are we to drink?" so Moses cried out to the Lord, and the Lord showed Moses a piece of wood. Moses threw the piece of wood into the water and the water became sweet (Exodus 15:22-25).

Marah (Heb) means – *bittersweet; grief; misfortune;* and *calamity.* Metaphysically Marah is the bitterness, trouble, sickness, and misery that those who pollute their minds with false beliefs and impure rebellious thoughts (thought-errors) bring upon themselves. It was at Marah, after the sweetening of the bitter waters that God declared,

There the Lord made a decree and a Law for them. He said, "If you listen carefully to the voice of the Lord your God and do what is right in his eyes, if you pay attention to his commands and keep all his decrees, I will not bring on you any of the diseases I brought on the Egyptians, for I am the Lord, who heals you." Exodus 15:25-26

Here is another test you will face in the wilderness. Each experience will be bitter-sweet. However, God says if you listen to his commands that He will not bring dis-ease upon you but will heal you. Follow the example of Moses. The water at first was bitter but when he added to it what God had told him it became sweet and drinkable. This should be a lesson: if things seem bitter, then God is probably not in it.

After the Israelites left Marah, they came to Elim, their second encampment, where there were twelve springs and seventy palm trees, and they camped there near the water (Exodus 15:26-27).

Elim (Heb.) means – A realization of fullness of life, strength, cleansing Truth and victory for the whole man. The number Twelve (12) represents fullness in the spiritual. Springs of water stand for life and cleansing. Oaks signify strength and protection, and palm trees denote victory. Once you start doing God's Will instead of self-will you will begin to project and attract attributes in your life such as strength, protection, and fullness of life.

Listening to the voice of God in every situation is the key to getting through the wilderness period. This is a time of building faith. We must stop listening to ourselves and to others and to those thoughts that are trying to get us to return to our old SELF. This will not be easy and as I said the response we get from our actions will be bitter-sweet.

Bread – Physical and Spiritual Food

Then the Lord said to Moses, "I will rain down bread from heaven for you. The people are to go out each day and gather enough for that day. In this way I will test them and see whether they will follow my instructions. Exodus 16:4

By now you have probably realized that the wilderness journey is a time of testing. This is the first of many tests that will come in the wilderness, and this is the Israelites first test of faith.

Bread has been called the food of life; it contains just about all the nutrients a body needs to survive. Just add water and we can survive for extended periods of time. In the Bible there are two kinds of bread: physical bread and spiritual bread. Jesus, as well as most scripture presents something physical to help explain something spiritual. It is easier that way because most people don't understand spiritual concepts, but they do understand physical ones.

In our discussion about bread there are five kinds of bread we will be explaining. Three of these breads have physical form and two do not. Remember, we are transitioning from the temporal, the material, and the physical to the permanent or spiritual, from the seen to the unseen.

The five breads are as follow:

<u>Physical Bread</u>

1. Bread – the physical body
2. Unleavened bread – the Passover bread
3. Manna – bread from heaven

<u>Spiritual Bread</u>

4. Bread – the body of Christ
5. Hidden Manna – hidden truths

Bread – the physical body

Up until this point our physical body, including our physical mind has "ate of" or "partook" of the sense-consciousness. It has been filled with false-thoughts, false -ideas and false-beliefs. Think of our mind and body as the dough and yeast as the false – teachings. This falsehood may give rise to the body, but it will eventually turn on it and destroy it. In the Gospel of

Matthew, Jesus warns us to guard against the teachings of the Pharisees and Sadducees.

"Be careful," Jesus said to them, "Be on your guard against, the yeast of the Pharisees and Sadducees." Matthew 16:6

His disciples finally understood what Jesus was saying,

Then they understood that he was not telling them to guard against the yeast used in bread, but against the teachings of the Pharisees and Sadducees." Matthew 16:12

To understand what Jesus meant by this, we first must understand the Pharisees and Sadducees literally and metaphysically. The Pharisees (Gk. from Heb.) *separatists; separated; distinct; accurate; literalist (separating word for word)*, were a Jewish sect, in the time of Jesus, who were religiously educated.

If you were not a member of their cult and didn't adhere to their religious beliefs and practices, you were regarded as strange or sinister no matter how good your works may have been. So, of course they considered Jesus an outsider and were opposed to his spiritual teachings.

The Pharisees went by "the letter of the law" (*literalist*) or the literal interpretation of the law and not by its spiritual meaning. When the law is enforced literally and not spiritually then it ends up defeating (killing) the very thing it intended to preserve.

He has made us competent as ministers of a new covenant – not of the letter but of the Spirit; for the letter kills, but the Spirit gives life. 2 Corinthians 3:6

Metaphysically, the Pharisee state of consciousness represents religious concepts that binds man to external forms of religion without knowing the reason for these particular forms and beliefs, and most importantly, not knowing their true spiritual meaning. The Pharisees, whether they were aware of the spiritual meaning or not didn't follow it nor did they explain it to the people.

Jesus said, "Woe to the Pharisees. Like a dog dozing in a food trough for cattle, they neither eat nor do they let the cattle eat." The Gospel of Thomas v.102

In my quest for the Truth, I found this Pharisee state of consciousness in most, if not all, of the churches I visited. If they had the Truth, they weren't sharing it and if you went outside of their teachings, you were definitely considered to be strange and sinister.

The doctrines and precepts that are founded on personal customs and traditions are profitless. To truly worship God, we must conform to an entirely new principle and teaching – Spirit and Truth.

Day after day every priest stands and performs his religious duties; again and again he offers the same sacrifices, which can never take away sins. Hebrews 10:11

Man's traditions are only symbols of God's real principles. Man's traditions are concerned with external formalities and customs lacking substance and Spiritual understanding. Most parishioners follow along as they're instructed never knowing or questioning the real reason behind the rituals they are performing. This excessive formalism leads to narrow-mindedness, bondage, and enslavement of its believers. It puts all the responsibility on God without the individual excepting any personal accountability, it is up to God to change us not for us to change ourselves.

Many know the Ten Commandments or the Mosaic Law and understand it literally and not spiritually. Take for instance, *'Thou shalt not commit adultery.'* We understand its meaning physically, but Jesus said that you have committed adultery even if you just look at someone in lust. Mosaic Law was given to prepare us for the coming Spiritual Law. If you are only concerned with the moral law, then you may not be following the Spiritual Law. Remember the Mosaic Law was given during the wilderness period or the time of transformation. The Mosaic Law was the temporary law until the permanent law was given.

In consciousness the "Pharisee" is a selfish state of mind. It is this self-satisfied mental attitude that causes the individual to lose sight of their body and souls spiritual needs. When we believe that religious traditions and rituals will change us, we render the Word of God ineffective. This is why the Pharisees, and many people today reject Jesus for he was the Word incarnate.

There are probably more Pharisees' today than in the time of Jesus. Those who give more attention to the forms of religious rites become unbalanced, losing sight of the true meaning behind the symbols, and are just going through the motions. They pretend to live a spiritual life but are lacking in Spiritual Truth. These are the true hypocrites. Those who's religious thoughts are established in traditions and rituals never miss an opportunity to argue with you and dispute every truth and new spiritual idea that you may present to them. They are keeping with "the letter of the law" and never consider its spiritual meaning. As with those who are like Jesus, the Pharisee's are always ready to crucify you.

(Jesus said), "You say, 'I am rich; I have acquired wealth and do not need a thing.' But you are wretched, pitiful, poor, blind, and naked." Revelation 3:17

The Pharisee consciousness is adverse to the Christ Consciousness, and the only way to eliminate this consciousness from our mind is to deny the world of symbols. The Pharisee consciousness can be overcome by receiving daily, new spiritual truths and by refusing to be bound by old religious thoughts. Jesus taught that the Kingdom of God would not come in an external form but can be found within us, yet Christians are constantly looking for the second coming of Christ.

They asked him, "When is the Kingdom coming?" He replied, "It is not coming in an easily observable manner. People will not be saying, 'Look, its over here' or 'Look, it's over there.' Rather, the Kingdom of the Father is already spread out on the earth, and people aren't aware of it." The Gospel of Thomas v.113

When we understand the spirit of the law it overthrows the outer forms of worship. Those who are strict in observing the letter of the law oppose the spirit of the law thus they miss the truth of the Higher Self that exists within each and every one of us. They don't recognize that we are the Kingdom of God.

It is the Christ Mind that saves us from our sorrows and distress that is brought on by condemning others for their non-traditional beliefs. When the Christ Consciousness comes, the individual becomes merciful and forgiving, not condemning.

The pharisaical mind interprets scripture literally and personalize God, the Devil, and Satan, localizes heaven and hell, and looks to the outside for 'signs and wonders,' not comprehending that internally establishing Truth in consciousness causes one to become aware of the Kingdom.

Simon Peter answered, "You are the Christ [Messiah], the Son of the living God." Jesus replied, "Blessed are you, Simon son of Jonah, for this was not revealed to you by man, but by my Father in heaven." Matthew 16:16-17

Those who come into the spiritual understanding and practice of Truth outgrow their old traditional beliefs that forms and ceremonies are necessary in religious worship.

(Jesus replied) "Woe to you experts of the law, because you have taken away the key to knowledge. You yourselves have not entered, and you have hindered those who were entering." Luke 11:52

The Pharisees were always trying to trip Jesus up and humiliate him publicly. This is true even today that those who are of the Pharisee state of mind are constantly trying to find some discrepancy in the new consciousness; lying in wait to pour their traditional beliefs on others. The coldness and hardness of their formal religion seeks to kill out the understanding of divine love and wisdom if it only could.

And they could not take hold of his words before the people: and they marveled at his answer and held their peace. Luke 20:26 (KJV)

Unleavened Bread – the Passover Bread

For seven days you are to eat bread made without yeast. On the first day remove the yeast from your houses, for whoever eats anything with yeast in it from the first day through the seventh must be cut off from Israel. Exodus 12:15

All our lives, we have fed off of the teachings and wisdom of a world full of falsehood and lies. Now it is time to start feeding off the knowledge and wisdom of God. In Egypt the Israelites ate the Passover Bread, Unleavened Bread, or bread without yeast. Our first step in purifying the body is to remove all the false teachings (yeast) from entering our life.

This will not be easy some of these false ideas have been burned into our brain, but we must turn our back on the world and all its falsehood. We were raised to be of the world, to have a good job, to have a family and enjoy all the material things that this world has to offer. Most people see material possessions as a sign of success in life. I once heard it said that the man with the most toys at the end wins. However, by now you've realized that material possession will not make you happy.

The Unleavened Bread or bread without any worldly additives is what is needed to get us through to the new consciousness. Mixing spiritual truths with worldly lies is considered to be spiritual adultery, so we must avoid this from happening. If the yeast filled bread is the Conscious-Life, then the Unleavened Bread is the Passover Bread from the conscious mind to the spiritual mind.

The Passover Bread or Unleavened Bread contains no worldly teachings (yeast), it is a bread of asking no questions and following directions. During your Passover it is best that you listen to what your Moses-ego is telling you and follow the voice within. You will have plenty of time to ask questions later. For now, it is best to hide behind the inner door or that door that leads to the subconscious and let the death angel pass by. You are starting to rid yourself of falsehood and you don't need someone who is still worldly filling you back up with lies.

Manna – bread from heaven

The people of Israel called the bread manna. Exodus 16:31

The word "manna" is based on the Hebrew word "man," which means "gift." Therefore, manna was a gift from God. Manna is the bread from heaven or the spiritual food of the subconscious. Remember that the subconscious is the soul-mind and manna is the bread that gives life to our soul. Manna is the spiritual and mental bread that we need to partake of daily to nourish us on our wilderness journey.

Manna is divinely supplied spiritual nourishment. It can also be referred to as spiritual energy that gives us strength and power and is the true source of strength and power that comes from the Word of God.

Jesus answered, *"It is written: 'Man does not live on bread alone, but on every word that comes from the mouth of God.'"* Matthew 4:4 (Deuteronomy 8:3)

It is the Word living in us or the light (knowledge of God) that our soul will respond to. It is the Word of God that penetrates through to the sub-conscious and to the mind of the soul. Just as the physical body needs to be fed daily our soul or sub-conscious needs to be fed as well. Before you fed only on worldly things, and they made your soul sick. The soul is spiritual, and it needs to feed off spiritual energy. In the universe there are entities that feed off negative energy just as there are entities that feed off positive energy. But in the kingdom of heaven, the universe of God, the entities feed on spiritual energy. If we are spiritual beings having a physical experience, then we must feed the physical body in which we incarnate but we also must feed the spiritual body. If not the two will become dis-eased.

Jesus said, "Woe to the flesh dependent on the soul; woe to the soul dependent on the flesh." The Gospel of Thomas v.112

The physical body is not keeping the soul alive, and the soul is not keeping the physical body alive. They both must be fed to survive.

One of the hardest lessons you will have to learn in the wilderness is to be thankful each day for the "manna" or gift of spiritual energy that is provided. Being thankful through our trust and humility, for whatever occurs to us mentally, spiritually, and physically keeps the way cleared for us on our way to the Promised Land. Remember God despises murmuring.

The manna (spiritual energy) is to be gathered daily. This is another wilderness test to see if you are obedient to the Word of God. We are to give thanks and praise daily as we receive our daily portion of spiritual energy that is essential in feeding our mind, body, and soul. Spiritual energy is not to be taken all at once, it is too powerful for the mortal mind and body to contain. Like the manna that the Israelites consumed it is to be gathered daily. Any manna that was left over spoiled by the following day. The spiritual energy or spiritual inspiration that is needed for today may not be the same spiritual inspiration needed for tomorrow. So don't think that what you receive today you save for another day. No, it is to be consumed the day it is given.

To receive our daily bread is to prepare us for the journey ahead and remind us not only to be thankful for times when we have plenty but also to be thankful in the days when we are given only what is sufficient for the day. The spiritual manna builds our trust in God that He will not only provide strength and energy needed for today but will also provide the strength and energy we will need for tomorrow.

Bread – the Body of Christ

Then Jesus declared, "I am the bread of life. He who comes to me will never go hungry, and he who believes in me will never go thirsty. John 6:35

The fourth bread or the Body of Christ is just that the Christ Consciousness.

He (Jesus) told them still another parable: "The Kingdom of Heaven is like yeast that a woman took and mixed into a large amount of flour until it worked all through the dough." Matthew 13:33

The flour or teachings of Christ (The Word) are added to our life, and they have to work their way through our consciousness – mind, body, and soul. When we are fully mixed with the Creative Forces it will give rise to the "hidden manna," the fifth bread or fifth level of consciousness. This fifth level of consciousness is as far as we can go in this earth plane.

Bread as the body of Christ represents spiritual substance or spiritual understanding which makes up the Body of Christ. Sub means "under," and stance means "stand" or to "understand." A body gives material form to something abstract. Abstract means existing in thought or as an idea but not having a physical or concreate existence. Spiritual understanding is what makes the Christ concrete or exist in material or physical form. Without spiritual understanding the Christ makes no sense to most, but to understand ourselves and to understand God more fully we must first understand the Christ.

Every day they continued to meet together in the temple courts. They broke bread in their homes and ate together with glad and sincere hearts, praising God and enjoying the favor of all the people. And the Lord added to their number daily those who were saved. Acts 2:46-47

In our consciousness the breaking of bread is the concentrating of our mind upon the real possession or the inner substance of Spirit. For those who attain the understanding of Christ (*those who were saved*) will testify to the joy (*with glad and sincere hearts*) with which it is appropriated in their consciousness. All outward pleasures can't compare with the inner light of the Holy Spirit when it sheds its rays on our heart.

The Christ is the I AM or God invisible. In the Old Testament, the I AM, was called Jehovah. Christ is the Perfect-Son idea that exists in all of us. It was the man Jesus that brought the Christ into expression and instructs us to do the same.

(Jesus answered), "I am the bread of life. Your forefathers ate the manna in the desert, yet they died. But here is the bread that comes down from heaven, which a man may eat and not die. I am the living bread that came down from heaven. If anyone eats of this bread, he will live forever. This bread is my flesh, which I will give for the life of the world." John 6:48-51

Once we reach the Christ or our true Higher Self, we realize our divine origin and birth. When we continually combine our thoughts with the Christ Consciousness, we will be the sons that God intended and manifest His consciousness in the world as did Jesus.

Jesus said, "When you understand yourselves you will be understood. And you will realize that you are Sons of the living Father. If you do not know yourselves then you exist in poverty and you are that poverty." The Gospel of Thomas v.3b

At this point I hope you are starting to understand the necessity of The Wilderness Steps and are beginning to see the transformation taking place. This was the transformation of the disciples of Jesus. He transformed their thoughts and minds from the limited to the unlimited; from the temporal to the permanent; from the material to the spiritual.

Today as in Jesus' day, Christians are looking for Jesus to return and change the world. Jesus changed the world by giving us a glimpse of the real world, the true reality. God's world is true, and the world that man has made is a lie and false reality. God doesn't want to change the false reality He wants it to end, and it ends when we start believing in the Truth, the truth that the world in which we live is false and an illusion of our own making.

They exchanged the truth of God for a lie and worshiped and served created things rather than the Creator – who is forever praised. Amen. Romans 1:25

In the Gospel of Matthew, the Kingdom of Heaven is likened to yeast or truth that is introduced to an individual. At first the truth is just a thought in mind but eventually works its way through the whole body like the yeast that makes its way through the dough to make it rise. In the Gospel of Thomas, it is the woman who is likened to the Kingdom rather than the yeast. She is putting the yeast or teaching into the dough (body).

Jesus said, *"The Kingdom of the Father is like a woman who took a little leaven and concealed it in dough. She made large loaves of bread. He who has ears let him hear."* The Gospel of Thomas v.96

In the Gospel of Thomas, a lot of the sayings point to the person as the central simile that is likened to the Kingdom of God. It is the person that is up and doing something. At first, we may be introduced to these new and exciting truths but once it makes its way through our consciousness it is now our duty to introduce these truths to others.

For example, "Christ is the message; Jesus is the messenger."

Hidden Manna – hidden truths

He who has an ear, let him hear what the Spirit says to the churches. To him who overcomes, I will give some of the hidden manna. Revelation 2:17

During the Exodus the Israelites were fed manna, the bread from heaven which sustained them during their wilderness journey. Once we reach the higher consciousness or spiritual understanding it is the Christ Consciousness that sustains us. It is the Christ Consciousness that is the spiritual sustenance needed to strengthen and sustain us in the Promised Land or the permanent condition.

Jesus said to them, "I tell you the truth, it is not Moses who has given you the bread from heaven, but it is my Father who gives you the true bread from heaven. For the bread of God is he who comes down from heaven and gives life to the world." John 6:32-33

Manna is the physical version of the spiritual hidden manna. The seen and the unseen spiritual truths. The physical is the result of a spiritual activity, it is cause and effect or sowing and reaping. Spirit is the cause, the physical or material is the effect. You see the physical and material and you believe this to be reality, but it is not. It is only the shadow of reality or just an illusion. This is part of the transitioning period, converting the seen back into the unseen. Once this has taken place you will see the true realty – the Kingdom of God.

The sense conscious, personal conscious, and the carnal conscious are all part of the illusion. These consciousness' are not real and therefore not eternal. It is only the Christ Consciousness or Spiritual Consciousness that is real and eternal. One may live off physical and material manna for a period of time, but it will not sustain them. Only when we partake of the hidden manna will we live forever.

Those Who Overcome

In the first three chapters of the book of Revelation Jesus is speaking to the seven churches of Asia. What I find interesting is that Jesus is pointing out the church's virtues and their sins (errors). Ephesus was the leading church of the seven and where the Apostle Paul spent many years preaching the Gospel of Christ with much success. It is said that these seven churches represent a history of the church and its modern condition.

The church teaches that Jesus died for our sins and if this is true then why is he making the seven churches aware of their sins and tells them that they must overcome them? I guess that's a discussion for another day.

Jesus not only pointed out each church's sins he also gave each a promise if they could overcome them. I want you to view these seven churches not only as seven stages in the history of the church but also to understand that the sins and promises pertain to us individually. After all who is the church. We are!

For those members of the church of Ephesus that overcome the *'loss of love'* and *'backsliding,'* Jesus says that he will give the right to eat (or partake) of the tree of life, which is in the paradise of God. The whole purpose of the awakening is to return us to that time and state of consciousness (Paradise) that existed before the fall or separation of the Sons of God from the Father. Paradise is the state of consciousness in which all of our being believes only in the 'good.' This was the condition in the Garden of Eden, the goodness of God. Remember what Jesus did on the cross, he restored the condition of good when he said to the thief, the one who believed in Christ, that today he would be with Jesus in Paradise.

Then he said, "Jesus, remember me when you come into your kingdom." Jesus replied, "I tell you the truth, today you will be with me in paradise!" Luke 23:42-43

When we reach the Christ Consciousness, we will affirm the good to be all that exists, and we will begin to express and manifest the good in our life and in our world.

The second church is Smyrna, where Jesus says to those who can overcome *'no reproof'* or no expression of blame or disapproval, will be given the *'the Crown of Life'*. The Crown of

Life or the Martyrs Crown is for those individuals who stood the testing in the wilderness and remained steadfast under trial.

The third church is Pergamum. Jesus says to those who overcome *'tolerance of wrong doctrines and heretics'* will be given *'hidden manna'*. Hidden manna is inner knowledge or hidden understanding within us that is only revealed when we reach a higher more logical and sensible way of thinking or reasoning.

The fourth church is Thyatira. Jesus says to those who overcome *'lax discipline,'* and *'tolerance of the corruption of those who speak on behalf of God,'* will be given, *'...authority over the nations'*. Authority over nations represents having authority or self-control over one's own thoughts, emotions, and feelings.

The fifth church is Sardis. Those who overcome *'extreme formalism'* and *'inactivity,'* Jesus says, will walk with him dressed in white and their names will not be blotted out of the book of life. White represents purity and the aura of Spirit. Formalism is the strict adherence to external forms in religion such as rituals and traditions that miss the point where God is concerned. Formalism shifts one's focus away from the internal spiritual and ethical principles of God toward the outward forms that embody that particular religion. Formalism diverts one's attention and affections from the important to the unimportant or as scripture says – from the wine to the wineskins.

Jesus used the metaphor of the new wine and old skins, to illustrate why he did not lead his disciples to follow the religion of the Pharisees, specifically in fasting. The Pharisees' rules were like old wineskins, brittle and inflexible. When these old skins were filled with new wine, they would break apart. Similarly, those who hold to old beliefs and ideas are intolerant and inflexible towards new ideas.

The sixth church is Philadelphia. Those who *'keep my word,'* will be made a pillar in the temple of God and receive a new name. The pillars of the temple of God are 'Love and Peace.'

The seventh church is Laodicea. Those who overcome *'lukewarmness, spiritual conceit, no conscious need, spiritual poverty, and spiritual blindness,'* will have the right to sit with Jesus on his throne just like he has the right to sit next to the Father because he has overcome.

Spiritual poverty is when someone is rich in money or material possessions, but not towards God. The Church of Laodicea was the *'rich but poor church,'* rich but complacent in their self-satisfaction, never realizing that the presence of Christ is not with them anymore.

Complacency is the root of spiritual poverty. Complacency is a state of listless passivity, a 'lukewarm' condition, finding comfort in mediocrity and the status quo while indulging in one's own whims as your passion for God fades away.

For the waywardness of the simple will kill them, and the complacency of fools will destroy them; but whoever listens to me will live in safety and be at ease, without fear of harm. Proverbs 1:32-33

A lukewarm faith that is neither hot nor cold is useless. The followers of Christ are called to action not a 'no conscious need' attitude.

(Jesus said), "I know your deeds, that you are neither cold nor hot. I wish you were either one or the other! So, because you are lukewarm – neither hot nor cold – I am about to spit you out of my mouth." Revelation 3:15-16

I mention the churches because I want you to see the sins and rewards of those who transition from the temporal to the permanent consciousness:

<u>Sins or Errors</u>	<u>God's Promises</u>
Loss of Love	The Tree of Life
No Reproof	Crown of Life
Tolerance of Wrong Doctrines	Hidden Manna

Lax Discipline   Authority
Extreme Formalism, Inactivity   Purity
Not Keeping the Word   Pillar in the Temple of God
Lukewarm   Acceptance

The Meaning of the Seven Churches

Ephesus (Gk.) *desiring; appealing* – represents the central building faculty of the consciousness called 'desire.' In the regenerative man, desire is often directed towards sensory and physical ideas, but it must be elevated to a higher level of consciousness. This is accomplished through the Word of God. Desire is the force or energy, which makes just about everything happen. Desire can lead to new and better things, but it can also lead to trouble and despair.

Smyrna (Gk. from Heb.) *distilling* – represents understanding and is the substance center of consciousness. Substance is the gist or main idea of something. If you remember the main point of a lesson, you've got the substance. Distilling is the fact or process of extracting the essential meaning or most important aspects of something.

Pergamum (Gk.) *strongly united* – represents the intellectual consciousness or decision-making faculty which can be swayed by the mind and emotions when we make decisions based on feelings rather than on logic. Within the soul exists two facilities, the intellect and the will which are closely knit. The intellect is the understanding part of our soul and while the will is the decision-making part of our soul or subconscious.

The intellect presents information to the will and the will then decides what to act upon or not act upon. With more understanding the better our decision making.

Thyatira (Gk.) *rushing headlong* – represents the intense desire of the soul for the higher expression of life. Zeal or enthusiasm (intense and eager enjoyment, interest, or approval) in pursuit of a cause or an objective is the central thought. Zeal or enthusiasm is not a bad thing unless we become zealous for both the sense and the spiritual consciousness. Mixing these two together is considered 'adultery.' To commit adultery is to put these two lines of thought into action. Again, one is real, and the other is not. They will always be at odds with one another.

Sardis (Gk.) *carnelian* – represents the desire for power. The question is are we exercising power and dominion over our thoughts or are we giving up power to our sense desires, passions, and appetites?

Carnelian is a stone that connects to the lower chakras. This means that it brings the metaphysical properties of being a gem that offers stability, grounding, a zest for life, and helps improve confidence and creativity.

Philadelphia (Gk.) *brotherly love* – represents the love center or love expression in consciousness. The love center is the assembly of I AM love thoughts that make up the love faculty that is essential to mental or physical power. If the Assembly of love thoughts are given over to selfishness they become *'the synagogue of Satan'*. Selfish love thinks that it is real love, but it is not. Loss of love causes the "trial" that is coming upon the inhabitants of Earth. From the synagogue of Satan comes strife, hatred, and warring thoughts. Love will harmonize the warring conditions in our own consciousness and in all the Earth, but harmony begins in the individual. Out of love comes peace.

Laodicea (Gk.) *justice of the people; judgment of the people* – represents a phase of the judgment faculty that an individual expresses in their personal life. In this phase of judgment, the individual bases their understanding, and their decision-making on what appears to be real or true but may not necessarily be so.

These are the things that must be overcome during the Wilderness Steps:

1. Ephesus – Selfish desire
2. Smyrna – False understanding
3. Pergamum – Illogical reasoning
4. Thyatira – Over enthusiasm (zealous)
5. Sardis – Personal power and influence
6. Philadelphia – False Love
7. Laodicea – Critical judgment

Transitioning from the temporal to the permanent takes time, patience, and effort on the part of the individual. The perfection of the individual will not be completed until the personal consciousness and ego is let go.

Hanging On

As the wilderness journey continued the Israelites began to murmur even more. Some Jewish scholars claim that the real complainers among the children of Israel were not the Israelites but the Egyptian "hangers-on" who also followed Moses. These Egyptians were not content in their own land and seized the opportunity to escape their fate by joining Moses and the Israelites.

The Israelites most likely had faith in Moses and never questioned his guidance. Unlike the Egyptians, who were used to having material forms as images to worship. The Israelites were more familiar with their God as Spirit. The Egyptians needed the seen, the physical and the material to reassure them. They needed the miraculous to realize that the Israelite God was to be experienced rather than seen.

As you continue The Wilderness Steps you will have feelings and emotions of your past life in the world (Egypt) that keep hanging on. You will also have those around you that don't want to take the responsibility of freeing their own souls but will try to 'piggy-back' their way through. They will murmur, grumble, and whine without having a serious complaint. This can't happen so don't try to carry them with you. Each individual has to make their own decision and have to experience God for themselves. So don't allow others to influence you especially if you know that they are not on the same spiritual journey that you're on. They may seem knowledgeable, but they lack wisdom because they have never experienced a time alone with God. I think that God hates murmuring more than any sin. No one likes a whiner.

These men (godless men) are grumblers (murmurers) and faultfinders; they boast about themselves and flatter others for their own advantage. Jude 16

And just as dangerous is to try to bring someone along with you. They are not on the same level of consciousness or completed the steps that you have. It is tempting to have someone with you on your journey, but this is not a partnership it is an individual quest. What will happen is that instead of them coming along they will only hold you back. Letting go of yourself also includes letting go of anyone or anything that has attached, or desires to be attached to you.

Water from the Rock

So they quarreled with Moses and said, "Give us water to drink." Moses replied, "Why do you quarrel with me? Why do you put the Lord to the test?" Exodus 17:2

As the Israelites stayed on the move, they also stayed on Moses back. When they reached Rephidim to make camp, there was no water to drink. To show you that the steps you are following are being reversed and what has been done is being undone, the three tests that the Israelites failed miserably in the wilderness is the same three things that Satan tempted Jesus with after Jesus had fasted for forty days, which is symbolic of the 40-year wilderness period.

Here are the three sins or errors made by the Israelites in the wilderness and Moses' reply:

1. They complained they had no food to eat. (Exodus 16)

   He humbled you, causing you to hunger and then feeding you with manna, which neither you nor your fathers had known, to teach you that man does not live on bread alone but on every word that comes from the mouth of the Lord. Deuteronomy 8:3

2. They tested God because they had no water to drink. (Exodus 17)

   Do not test the Lord your God as you did at Massah. Deuteronomy 6:16

3. They worshipped the golden calf. (Exodus 32)

   Fear the Lord your God, serve him only and take your oaths in his name. Do not follow other gods, the gods of the peoples around you. Deuteronomy 6:13

Here are Satan's three temptations to Christ Jesus during Jesus' wilderness experience and Jesus' Old Testament reply (Matthew 4):

1. "If you are the son of God, tell these stones to become bread."

   Jesus answered, "It is written 'Man does not live on bread alone, but on every word that comes from the mouth of God.'" Matthew 4:4 (Deuteronomy 8:3)

2. If you are the son of God throw yourself off the highest point of the temple for it is written the angels will lift

you in their hands so that you will not strike your foot against a stone.

Jesus answered, "It is also written: 'Do not put the Lord your God to the test.'" Matthew 4:7 (Deuteronomy 6:16)

3. All the kingdoms of the world I will give you if you bow down and worship me.

   Jesus said to him, "Away from me, Satan! For it is written: 'Worship the Lord your God and serve him only.'" Matthew 4:10 (Deuteronomy 6:13)

Notice the response by Jesus is the same response by Moses.

I need you to understand this. What you have done must be undone. What man has done must be undone. This was the purpose of Jesus (the last man), to undo the errors that Adam (the first man) had done. The purpose of The Prodigal Steps and The Wilderness Steps is to undo the errors that we have done. I use the term "error" instead of the word "sin," because sins may be forgiven but it doesn't mean they have been undone. The whole purpose of reincarnation is to undo the errors one has made in a previous life or lives. Errors can be corrected or reversed by doing the opposite. In the Prodigal Steps, I show how, for example to reverse step five – Spiritual Destruction, one must complete step ten – Repentance.

The three temptations are one of the errors that Jesus had to undo. The Israelites failed to overcome these three errors, but Jesus showed us how they can be overcome by following the Word of God.

Just like the Israelites you are hungry and thirsty for answers. But continuing to murmur will only bring trouble. Moses was led by God to a rock at Horeb. There, Moses struck the rock with the same staff with which he struck the Nile and turned the water to blood. The staff of Moses represents the authority of God. Literally, you have the power of God in your hand, you just don't realize it yet.

The place that Moses struck the rock, he called Massah and Meribah, which means testing and quarreling. The Israelites tested the Lord by saying, "Is the Lord among us or not?" At this point in your wilderness journey, you are probably asking the same question, "Where is God?" Have faith the Lord will show up.

Horeb (Heb.), *dryness; desert; desolation; solitude,* is a state of higher spiritual realization this is attained by affirming the power and presence of divine substance and nourishment that is within us. The purpose of these steps is to bring you to the realization that what your soul hungers and thirsts for is not from the outside world but from the Spirit within. To find it, we must go into the solitude of the inner mind, there we will come into conscious union with the divine. The Israelites didn't feel the presence of God because they were looking outwardly to find Him.

The Amalekites

Amalek (Heb.) *warlike; dweller in the vale; valley dweller; that licks up.*

The first battle the Israelites had to fight in the wilderness was against the Amalekites. Some biblical sources say Amalek was a descended from Ham, the son whose seed was cursed by Noah and other sources say that Amalek was probably the grandson of Esau, the son of Isaac who sold his birthright for pottage (Genesis 25:29-34).

The Amalekites are a kind of archenemy of Israel (the seeker). Whenever the Amalekites are mentioned in the Bible it is in connection with raids, bloodshed, and violence. They were the first nation to make war on Israel. This battle occurred immediately after the Israelites left Rephidim, a time when

Israel was at its weakest. The Amalekites' objective of the raid was to capture the well that had miraculously appeared for Moses at Horeb. The raid on the Israelites shows the Amalekites disregard for God's Will and purpose.

Metaphysically 'the valley' symbolizes the subconscious mind. As *"valley dwellers,"* Amalek and his descendants signify lust, a force which is warlike and destructive in nature and, when established in the animal forces of man's subconscious, is the begetter of destructive and rebellious appetites and passions.

Amalek was the son of Eliphaz (Heb.) *God is purification; God is strength; whom God makes strong*, thus desire at its origin is good and of God; but when it is misdirected by the carnal man it becomes lust, *"he that licks up"* or he who consumes.

Eliphaz, son of Esau, was one of the three men who came to Job after Satan tried to destroy his life (Job 2). Eliphaz, the Temanite, signifies thoughts that spring from the subconscious of strength and purification (*God is strength; God is purification*). However, these thoughts do not measure up to Spiritual Truth but are capable of unfolding into greater understanding and fruitfulness. Even though Eliphaz offered encouragement to Job, he didn't feel he could help his friend.

The Amalekites represent man's base desires, his animal forces, appetites, and passions. The desires are warlike and destructive in nature and must be eliminated and forever denied a place in our consciousness. It is easy to see why Moses pronounced a perpetual war on Amalek, and why the prophet Samuel later commanded king Saul (the first king of Israel) to destroy the Amalekites and totally annihilate everything that belonged to them, including their men, women, children, and even their animals (1 Samuel 15). Metaphysically, the Amalekites (lust & desire) are an ever-present threat and enemy to the Spirit within. If we don't completely put an end to all of these thought-errors eventually they will go to war with us.

The Israelites may have won the battle against the Amalekites, but they were not completely destroyed. King Saul also failed to totally annihilate the Amalekites. King Saul disobeyed God's directive and spared king Agag and the best of the sheep and cattle. Because of Saul's disobedience God told Samuel (priest, first prophet and last judge in Israel) that He was grieved that He had appointed Saul king of Israel. Samuel went to Saul and told him what God said to him. Saul defended himself by saying that he had defeated the Amalekites as God had instructed but saved the best of their animals to later sacrifice to God. Samuel said for king Saul to 'stop' and listen to what God had said to him,

(Samuel said). *"The Lord anointed you king over Israel. And he sent you on a mission, saying, 'Go and completely destroy those wicked people, the Amalekites; make war on them until you wiped them out.' Why did you not obey the Lord? Why did you pounce on the plunder and do evil in the eyes of the Lord?'"* 1 Samuel 17-19

I spent some time here on the Amalekites because I want you to understand the message here. The Amalekites represent our selfish desires that if not eliminated entirely and totally from our mind will keep coming back to try and destroy us. Joshua and his army did not destroy them, Saul and his army did not destroy them and eventually king David and his army went to war with them.

Obedience to the Lord (divine law) will bring peace and joy to our lives and lead to paths of pleasantness and prosperity. Disobedience will lead to dis-ease and despair. If you don't subdue your thought-errors and gain dominion over them they will keep coming back again and again.

King Saul said he saved the best of what the Amalekites possessed. There is nothing good about selfishness and selfish desire that is worth saving. Disobedience comes in many forms and the most stubborn are those who refuse to obey. They stand up for their false ideas believing that what they are doing is necessary, but what they believe necessary is mostly for themselves. They tell themselves that certain things are good for us, that man has always indulged in these thought-errors. Overtime these false ideas have become fixed in consciousness. They are not receptive to the Spirit of Truth and refuse to give up their position of power. As Samuel said the Lord will be dealing with these false idea's generation after generation.

Samuel asked Saul if the Lord delights more in sacrifice or obedience. This is the main lesson here and the same question that is being asked to you – sacrifice or obedience? The test in the wilderness is "Are you obedient to God," but mostly do you have faith in God, and do you trust him?

Be careful to follow every command I am giving you today, so that you may live and increase and may enter and possess the land that the Lord promised on oath to your forefathers. Remember how the Lord your God led you all the way in the desert these forty years, to humble you and to test you in order to know what was in your heart, whether you keep his commands. Deuteronomy 8:1-2

Why does God kill people?

God told the Israelites time and time again to go and kill. Do you think God today tells anyone to go and kill someone or people? Let's be real here and look at the facts. The Bible says that God's purpose for the earth is for it to be His footstool and whatever stands in the way of this must eventually be eradicated.

The symbolism of the footstool is that the king's enemies have been thoroughly defeated, and completely at the mercy of the victorious king. The imagery of Jesus using his enemies as a footstool means that he is victorious over them, and they are now completely under his control.

Because of the way the Amalekites conducted themselves and the way they treated their servants they were considered by God to be unclean beasts and were an abomination to the Promised Land, therefore, before the Israelites could enter, the Amalekites had to be eradicated in fear that they would contaminate the Israelites with their lewd behavior and lack of respect for God.

I find it interesting that it was said of the Amalekites that they were sorcerers who to avoid being captured could transform themselves to resemble animals. This may be why God had Samuel instruct king Saul to destroy all the livestock. The presence of the Amalekites threatened everything that God accomplished thus far. The Israelites were already behind schedule in reaching the Promised Land and further setbacks were not in God's plans.

God said that he would completely destroy the Amalekites and the only way this prophecy may have been fulfilled was if the Amalekites repented and changed their ways. But this did not happen. It has been said of God that He will not always wink at the wickedness of a nation. Let this be a warning to all of us, there is coming a time, and not only in America, that we will all have to pay for our selfishness. Remember the earth is God's footstool, no nation 'gets by' with anything anymore than an individual does.

There are some individuals and even nations today that are considered Amalekites. They are influenced and ruled by selfish desire and lust. When we light a match, we can see the flame until it burns out. But even when we no longer see the light, the radiation continues. We know that the good that we do will live on. That being said, the evil we do will also continue. As long as we allow our selfish desires and lusts to remain, there will always be an Amalekite state of consciousness, or at least until the Amalekites are officially gone. Don't be an Amalekite, their time is coming to an end.

Then the Lord said to Moses, "Write this on a scroll as something to be remembered and make sure that Joshua hears it, because I will completely blot out the memory of Amalek from under heaven." Exodus 17:14

Mount Sinai

Sinai (Heb.) – *deep ravines; cliff with ravines; precipitous* (dangerously high or steep); *sharp; jagged.*

Horeb (Heb.) – *dryness; drought; heat; waste; desolation; desert; barren; solitude.*

Moses and the Israelites camped at the mountain where he had the burning bush experience. The northern part of this mountain range is called Horeb and the southern part Sinai and in scripture is referred to as "the mountain of God" (Exodus 3:1).

This mountain of God symbolizes in us an exalted state of consciousness. Although this place in our mind may seem dangerous (*jagged; sharp*), let it be known that God is there. This state of high spiritual consciousness may seem precipitous and out of our reach, but it can be attained through affirming the presence and power of the inner I AM – Christ Consciousness. It is in solitude that we come into conscious union with the divine.

Horeb represents a high place in consciousness where we come into conscious union with the divine and can be attained if we affirm the power and presence of the one inner, divine sustenance and nourishment.

When Jethro, Moses's father-in-law, knew where Moses had settled, he came to see him with Zipporah, Moses's wife and his two sons (Exodus 18). Jethro was a descendant of Abraham and Keturah, and familiar with the form of worship and sacrifice taught by Abraham.

During Jethro's visit with Moses, he saw that he was too involved in the people's business having to personally make judgment over all their petty controversies and complaints. Jethro was able to make wise use of his abilities to counsel with the elders. He aided Moses in establishing the appointment of seventy men who were to be chiefs over thousands. They were to carry out all the detailed matters and leave Moses free for more important things.

The Lord uses everyone who is willing to be used. No man could do what Moses had to do unassisted. As a priest, no doubt Jethro was divinely guided. This is another lesson in the wilderness; we are to select capable men and women, who fear God and surround ourselves with them. They will serve as judges and will make our burdens lighter because they will share the load. But be careful of these capable men and women not all will make wise decisions. I found this to be true on my journey. I loved these people, but some were still very selfish and at times lacked good judgment.

Preparations to Meet the Lord

When the Lord told Moses he would speak to him on the mount, He gave Moses and the people three days to prepare themselves for the visitation (Exodus 9-11). Many of the Israelites did not make the preparations and consequently were not allowed to participate. If you fail to make preparations for your wilderness journey, you may also be denied participation and entry into the Promised Land.

To prepare for the Lord's visitation Moses relayed the message he had received from God and told the Israelites how to prepare themselves.

1. Remember what God had done to Egypt.
2. Obey God and fully keep His covenant.
3. The people were to be consecrated by washing their clothes and abstaining from sexual relations.

4. They were not to go up the mountain or touch the foot of it, or they would be put to death.

The Israelites had only three days to prepare, and this may have a symbolic meaning of the three days of Jesus' death, burial, and resurrection. Only two men, Moses and Aaron were able to ascend the mountain.

Until you have cleansed your mind and your body you will not be able to go up the mountain and commune with God. In preparation, it may be easy to clean your clothes, but I believe it refers to cleansing not only the body but also the mind. Abstaining from sexual relations may be more difficult and impossible for some. When I was at this point in my own wilderness journey, I went five years without having sexual relations. I'm not saying you have to go this long but five represents the five senses and it was all of my five senses that were involved in my sexual relationships. Also, remember from where you came – the pigpen. But most importantly remember obedience to God is more important than sacrifice.

To recognize something outwardly, it must first exist within us. For instance, to recognize hate in someone, we must first harbor feelings of hate. The same applies to love; we must embody love in order to feel it. To truly recognize the presence of God, one must be good and holy. How else would we recognize Him? This is why, in preparing to know cleanliness, we must first ensure purity in mind, body, and soul. This is why most people do not or have never felt the presence of God. Even if they have been in His presence, they would not have recognized Him because it is not within them to do so. God is Truth and to recognize the Truth we too must be truthful. God is merciful so we too must be merciful. This is the At-onement that my books talk about. This is what Jesus meant when he said I and the Father are one.

Patience

Patience is a virtue and was something that the Israelites didn't have. And this can also be said of us. Patience was never my strong suit. After Moses had been gone for 40 days and nights they gathered around Aaron and said,

When the people saw that Moses was so long in coming down from the mountain, they gathered around Aaron and said, "Come make us gods [or a god] who will go before us. As for this man Moses who brought us up out of Egypt, we don't know what has happened to him." Exodus 32:1

For a while your Moses-ego may leave you. This will be a trying time because you will be confused on what is next to come. It is another testing period to determine whether you will proceed with the journey or, like the Israelites, wish to return to your Egypt.

In The Godward Steps we are being shown the way, a perfect way, where we may cleanse our mind, body, and soul of our false ideas and beliefs. If this is the perfect way then why are we looking for another god, one made of gold, stone, metal, or wood to guide us? If we are patient and cleanse our self, then the spirit of Truth will manifest itself in our life.

In our zeal to find the truth, it may be our own zealousness that undermines the truth of our pursuit. However, if we are patient and stand still, we will begin to hear the quite, still voice within us. If we remain alert and aware, the 'signs of the way' will be revealed to us. Many people miss these signs because they are not paying attention; the distractions of the world consume them.

That's one of the purposes of my books: to make you aware of The Godward Steps and to help you recognize the signs. If you remove yourself from the equation and allow Him to guide you, without seeking through another channel, He has a way prepared for you.

(Jesus said), "Do not let your hearts be troubled. Trust in God, trust also in me. In my Father's house are many rooms; if it were not so, I would have told you. I am going there to prepare a place for you. And if I go and prepare a place for you, I will come back and take you to be with me that you may be where I am. You know the way to the place where I am going." John 14:1-4

It is best at this time not to rush into anything and definitely not behave like the Israelites and go back to worshipping the previous idols of Egypt. You may feel the need to find another mate, change jobs, or pursue other personal desires but God is at work preparing the way. Sometimes, this process may take time, so patience is the key. Rushing into decisions now could delay your journey through the wilderness.

The Lord's Presence

The Lord told Moses be careful that no one other than he and Aaron sets foot or even touches the mountain for whoever touches the mountain shall be put to death by being stoned or shot with arrows. Only when the rams horn sounded a long blast were they able to go up the mountain. On the morning of the third day Moses led the people out of the camp to meet with God. There was a thick cloud over the mountain and there was thunder and lightning as the Lord descended on it in fire.

The mountain was charged with electricity. The vibrations were raised so high, that those who were not attuned could not stand it. Moses put limits around the mountain and set it apart as holy to prevent sudden death to those who might accidently overstep the boundary. As the people stood at the foot of the mountain, they could hear the thunder and see the lighting. There was a very loud and long trumpet blast, and everyone trembled. Then Moses spoke and the voice of God answered him.

Then Moses led the people out of the camp to meet with God, and they stood at the foot of the mountain. Mount Sinai was covered with smoke, because the Lord descended on it in fire. The smoke billowed up from it like smoke from a furnace, the whole mountain trembled violently, and the sound of the trumpet grew louder. Then Moses spoke and the voice of God answered him [and God answered him with thunder]." Exodus 19:18-20

God called Moses up the mountain and instructed him to bring Aaron back down along with the priests, emphasizing that the people should not ascend to the Lord's presence, lest disaster befall them. (Exodus 19)

To merely adopt an attitude of prayer or undergo external purification is insufficient. Even those who cleansed themselves were still not permitted to meet the Lord. We must live in accord with what we are seeking – spirituality. We must be attuned to those vibrations which are necessary for receiving spiritually. This is what Jesus meant when he told us to ask in his name –not to ask just with words, but by living our lives as he lived his, at-one with the Father. If we do that, we can ask in his name, and it will be done.

After having prepared yourself for this time with God, you will not see God personally, but you may witness one of His miracles. This will happen to prove to you that God is real. Remember we are never not in the presence of God, He is always with us, so act accordingly.

STEP 12

Government | Unification

Government – *System to govern a state or community. A system of social control under which the right to make laws, and the right to enforce them, is vested in a particular group or society.*

Unification – *The process of being united or made into a whole.*

The Ten Commandments

Moses said to the people, "Do not be afraid. God has come to test you, so that the fear of God will be with you to keep you from sinning." Exodus 20:20

As the people saw and heard the power of God, they feared Him. They kept their distance and asked that Moses speak to them and not God because they were afraid, they would die.

It is well to picture in our minds how the Ten Commandments were given and who was with Moses at the time. The rest of the Bible is written around this chapter. Even the Sermon on the Mount, given by Christ, is just an extension of it.

The first three commandments pertain to our relationship to God, while the remaining seven focus on our relations with our fellow man.

<u>Law One</u>

"You shall have no other gods before [or besides] me." Exodus 20:3

No individual is to be considered before God. This is probably the most violated of all of God's commandments. This is why selfishness is so dangerous. Although we may not consider ourselves as idol worshippers, it is hard not to think first of ourselves and of our own wishes above all else. Self-preservation, Self-aggrandizement, Self-satisfaction, and Self-importance are just some of our self-troubles we face today as individuals and as a nation. We want what we want. We want to be all powerful; we want material possessions; we want money, fortune, and fame regardless of the cost. When our desires and our material possession are at stake can we really say to God, 'Your Will be done.' And truly mean it?

<u>Law Two</u>

"You shall not make for yourself an idol in the form of anything in heaven above or on the earth beneath or in the waters below. You shall not bow down to them or worship them; for I, the Lord your God, am a jealous God, punishing the children for the sin of the fathers to the third and fourth generation of those who hate me, but showing love to a thousand generation, of those who keep my commandments." Exodus 20:4

A graven image could be anything to which we have so much importance as to be all encompassing for us. It might be position, fame, money, prestige, or our cell phone for that matter. Any material desire that outweighs our desire to be a channel for God's manifestation and glorification is considered a graven image.

Non-Catholics feel that it is sinful to make a statue of the Virgin Mary. Orthodox Jews feel Christians are breaking the second commandment when they worship Jesus as the Christ. Yet they look on the patriarchs and prophets of old as messengers of God and examples to follow.

There is a difference between an object you worship and an example you live by. Jesus promised a day would come when we would worship God in Spirit and in Truth, but until we reach that state of consciousness, we will need constant reminders before us to help us reach the goal we are striving for.

What is meant by a jealous God? It is necessary at times to use certain words to convey certain meanings. Jealousy was and is only another way of saying, *'What you sow, so shall you reap'*. It indicates certain laws are set in motion according to our actions, which bring about definite results.

Punishing the children for the sins of their father to the third and fourth generations was refuted by some of the later prophets. Ezekiel disavowed the proverb that the fathers' consumption of sour grapes would cause their children's teeth to be set on edge. Instead, he emphasized that each soul was accountable for their own sins (Ezekiel 18). The concept of reincarnation might explain how a soul returns through multiple lives, reaching the third or fourth generation, to materially reap what it has sown.

<u>Law Three</u>

"You shall not misuse the name of the Lord, your God, for the Lord will not hold anyone guiltless who misuses his name." Exodus 20:7

Jesus said we should not swear by the temple (mind, body, and soul), for that is where God lives. When we say harsh things against others, it is the same as taking God's name in vain. We are all extensions of God, and everyone we meet should be regarded as our other self. We are all one in Christ and part of the Perfect-Son idea.

<u>Law Four</u>

"Remember the Sabbath day by keeping it holy. Six days you shall labor and do all our work, but the seventh day is a Sabbath to the Lord

your God. On it you shall not do any work, … For in six days the Lord made the heavens and the earth, … Therefore, the Lord blessed the Sabbath and made it holy." Exodus 20:8-11

Everyone must decide how they may best keep the Sabbath. God intended the Sabbath to be a day of rest but not only rest but a time of reflection to ponder His Word. The way we do this depends greatly upon our purpose and our place in this world. Rest does not mean just sitting around doing nothing it means changing the way we think about what we feel is right and what is good. And more importantly living up to it.

Law Five

"Honor thy father and mother, so that you may live long in the land the Lord your God is giving you." Exodus 20:12

To honor your parents is to think of them before yourself, showing them preference. If you truly honored your parents and respected them, you probably would desire to live longer, and your life would be in keeping with the purpose you had in entering this life.

Law Six

"Thou shall not kill (murder)." Exodus 20:13

Jesus told us that we can kill with anger. In fact, to kill 'one's spirit' with anger, a harsh word, pessimism, or any other form of negativity is a violation of this commandment. We are meant to be constructive and creative, not destructive. We should not destroy what we cannot give. The first command ever given was to be our brother's keeper (Genesis 4:9).

Law Seven

"Thou shalt not commit adultery." Exodus 20:14

Jesus' interpretation, of the seventh commandment refers not only to the physical act of adultery, but to any thought which would contaminate or separate us from the purity and spiritual unity for which we are striving.

<u>Law Eight</u>

"You shall not steal." Exodus 20:15

<u>Law Nine</u>

"You shall give false testimony against your neighbor." Exodus 20:16

<u>Law Ten</u>

"You shall not covet your neighbor's house. You shall not covet your neighbor's wife, or his manservant, his ox or donkey, or anything that belongs to your neighbor." Exodus 20:17

Laws 8, 9, & 10 are self-explanatory. We must remember that there are extremes in the material sense of the law, but not according to the spirit of the law as given by Jesus. In Christ all the extremes meet.

Reincarnation

The Laws of Moses are aimed at stopping or as least controlling man's self-indulgence, yet everything the Law forbade is still being practiced today such as incest, homosexuality, child-abuse, and not tending to the elderly and to those who are physically and mentally weak. Other offenses such as stealing, lying, oppression, dealing falsely, injustice to the poor, child prostitution, mediumship, wizardry, and intimidation of strangers are still ruling and ruining our society.

The law of God involves the orderly working out of His divine principles and ideals and expressing or manifesting these ideals in our lives and in our world. All the in-harmonies in the world that seem to be real are the result of man's false beliefs. Only spiritual things are real and eternal. These false beliefs may seem real but are only thought-errors that need to be eliminated from our mind. When we understand that God's creation is all there is, and knowing it to be good, the divine ideals are established in our mind and through the Law of Mind Action are brought forth and manifested in the earth plane.

Serving the Lord means keeping the divine law, and this includes right-thinking. Through the Law of Mind Action what men believe and what men think become what man beholds. We believe what we mentally see and see what we mentally believe whether true or not. The "heart" of man is his subconsciousness or his "soul". The divine law is written on man's heart and to save our soul we must meditate on and realize that spiritual ideas are the only true reality.

Man's false beliefs and thought-errors were from the beginning and way before the advent of man and these false beliefs and thought-errors have been passed down from generation to generation. Many of the pagan lines in the Promise Land were remnants of the pre-Adamic creation which had survived the Flood. The Nephilim or "giants" for instance, had superhuman physical ability, but lacked spiritual awareness. They were intent upon increasing their material strength, without thought of the spiritual source.

In the beginning, as the early thought-forms thought projected into the animal kingdom, a genetic code was created which preserved these forms in a physical way and were adopted by souls who were at that lower level of development. By eliminating these lines, or races, from the earth, Joshua was doing a service to these souls that they could not do for themselves. In their next incarnation, the giants were forced to take on bodies that were the result of the Adamic creation.

Hence reincarnation enables us to see the positive side of the pagan casualties in Israel's warfare, such as the Amalekites and giants. Perhaps by killing these people physically, spiritually Joshua was releasing their souls for greater opportunities, which they would not have had in their current bodies.

Jesus tells us,

"Do not be afraid of those who kill the body but cannot kill the soul. Rather, be afraid of the One who can destroy both soul and body in hell." Matthew 10:28

No doubt these creatures were already in hell, having descended from the mixture of thought-forms with the animal kingdom. With only having basic instincts like the animals they mixed with, they probably didn't know right from wrong. By killing their bodies, their souls were given another opportunity to reincarnate, thus providing them another chance to overcome their sins. When every purpose of an individual is to do evil, then the only opportunity for the soul is to be taken out of its dire condition – which means death. In that case, it is not unmerciful. To be absent from the body is to be present with God. So, who are we to judge God's judgment to send a flood to destroy these creatures? Through reincarnation, the individual has the opportunity to clean up their act and undo the atrocities that they have committed.

Death does not necessarily change the purpose of an individual for better or worse. I've heard those in the church say that when they die, they will be made perfect. Death doesn't have the power to make you perfect it merely gives us another chance to rid ourselves of selfishness. If it was true that the killing of evil individuals could wipe out sin, then the Flood would have overcome sin. God promised He would never again cut off all flesh by the waters of a flood. This was not the way. The evil influence cannot be overcome by physical means; it must be overcome by a change in the heart of man.

This is why God did not kill Cain after he murdered his brother. God knew that killing Cain would not end selfishness. As I have said before, our errors and mistakes must not only be forgiven but also undone and reversed so they will never exist again.

Now you understand the reason for Christ's coming to Earth: to show humanity that we must overcome sin within ourselves, as sin was the original cause of physical death. The wages of sin is death; therefore, we overcome death by our own spiritual evolution, not physical evolution.

What benefit did you reap at that time from the things you are now ashamed of? Those things result in death! But now that you have been set free from sin and have become slaves to God, the benefit you reap leads to holiness, and the result is eternal life. For the wages of sin is death, but the gift of God is eternal life in [or through] Christ Jesus our Lord. Romans 6:21-23

Murder

"Thou shall not kill (murder)." Exodus 20:13

In the fourth chapter of Genesis, is the first recorded death or murder of an individual due to the selfishness of another. After banishing Adam and Eve from paradise, God seemingly stayed nearby, keeping watch over them. He also established a form of redemption for their disobedience through a ritual of offering. The Bible says that Abel, the second son of Adam and Eve, brought as an offering to God, some of the fat portions of his flock. This must have been the correct or accepted method of offering. Cain worked in the soil or was a gardener or maybe a farmer and for his offering brought some of the fruits he had grown. This offering was unacceptable to God and thus God rejected Cains offering. This made Cain very angry.

Then the Lord said to Cain, "Why are you angry?" Why is your face downcast? If you do what is right, will you not be accepted?" But if you do not do what is right, sin is crouching at your door; it desires to have you, but you must master it." Genesis 4:6-7

Cain's name in Hebrew means, *selfishness; one who draws to itself.* Cain represents those who wish to acquire and possess things for themselves. Cain represents the flesh or the natural man. When Cain didn't get his way, he became angry. Anger is a sign of fear, and as the scripture says, fear is the first sign of sin or missing the mark. I would say that fear is one of the signs of selfishness (Cain).

Additionally, the scripture said that fear should be mastered thus to eliminate fear selfishness must be eliminated. Fear is something that exists in the Natural-man and will remain until he again becomes Spirit-man. Basically, selfishness is the fear of not getting what one thinks or believes they deserve.

The animal sacrifice approved by God as an offering probably goes back to Genesis chapter 3. After Adam and Eve disobeyed God by partaking of the Tree of Knowledge of Good and Evil, they felt ashamed and naked. In response, God made suitable clothing for them by killing an animal and creating *'coats of skin.'* Metaphysically these coats of skin or Hebrew "Chithanoth" which signifies not only coats but *body like; an embodiment; and expression of bodily form.*

The Lord God made garments of skin for Adam and his wife and clothed them. Genesis 3:21

Spirit-man was first associated with the spiritual, and it was only after he took on personal consciousness (sense-consciousness) was he given bodily form (coats of skin), which was more in keeping with a physical consciousness. God said that man was like us (spiritual) and must not be allowed to live forever in his new physical consciousness.

And the Lord God said, "The man has now become like one of us, knowing good and evil. He must not be allowed to reach out his hand and take also from the tree of life and eat and live forever. Genesis 3:22

But you say that later in the Bible man is to partake of the tree of life and become eternal. The flesh is corruptible and only when spiritualized will the corruptible body give way to the incorruptible body and the manifestation of the spiritual body. Until this happens the "Alter of Sacrifice" was set up as an example of how to reach the spiritual consciousness. The body or flesh must be sacrificed, not literally, but mentally. The corruptible flesh is a manifestation of corruptible ideas in mind. Accordingly, the incorruptible body is a manifestation of divine ideas.

*(Jesus said), "I will not speak with you much longer, for the prince of this world is coming. He has no hold over me, but the world must learn that I love the Father and that I do exactly what my Father has commanded me..."*John 14:30-31

Again, the purpose of my books is to show that what was done in error has to be undone. Adam and Eve's (mankind) selfish actions in the beginning must be undone before man is allowed back into Paradise. The corruptible must not be allowed to continue forever. By preventing Adam and Eve from partaking of the tree of life, death was introduced to slow the progression of selfishness.

Cain's anger led him to hate his brother and to eventually kill him. God accepted Abel's offering because it involved the sacrifice of an animal (representing the body), while Cain's offering of fruits indicates that sacrifice is more acceptable than offering first fruits or actions (deeds). Remember what is more acceptable to God – obedience over sacrifice.

Abel represents not the spiritual mind but the faculties in mind that control the animal functions in consciousness. When selfishness (Cain) kills the part of consciousness that keeps our animal instincts in check then the natural man is free to behave however he likes. This is why our animal side is to be mastered and controlled. If not, it may lead to murder and all sorts of depravity. For their survival, killing is the basic instinct and behavior of the animal kingdom.

As long as we live in the natural state of man, we are subject to both physical and spiritual laws. Natural-man is bound by the physical laws and subject to sense-thoughts and thus will always be in error or sinful. Spirit-man is free from these sense-thoughts and the world has no hold on him. Don't be tricked or forced in to satisfying your sense-thoughts. Others will try to pull out the natural man in you but don't give in to them.

Cain was not met with death for killing his brother, but rather he was banished to the Land of Nod and sentenced to a life of wandering. God said that He would never again kill the physical body. Without a body, the rebellious thought-forms have no way to correct their mistakes. God's purpose now is to give the children of God (thought-forms) time to come to their senses and realize the state of poverty in which they abide.

Cain took with him selfishness and embarked on the path of serving himself. The essence of selfishness, akin to the interpretation of Cain's name, leads to self-possession, self-aggrandizement, self-indulgence, and self-desire. Killing the body will not eliminate these thought-errors from consciousness. They must be replaced by or overcome by selfless thoughts.

The Substitute

Adam lay with his wife again, and she gave birth to a son and named him Seth, saying, "God has granted me another child in place of Abel, since Cain killed him." Genesis 4:25

The path of selfishness marked the onset of paganism. The Pagans were those who adhered to their own religious beliefs rather than those beliefs recognized by mainstream religions.

Essentially, they cared more about themselves than others. To help overcome this new form of consciousness, or the consciousness that feeds the senses, another path was established.

The third son of Adam and Eve was Seth. Seth in Hebrew means *settled; determined; founded; set; placed; constituted; disposed; substituted.* The idea of Seth would be the *substitute* for Abel or a substitute for the loss of the faculty of mind that controls man's animal behavior. Seth represents the movement to define the limits of something, to establish it, found it, and dispose of it. In this case we are speaking of selfishness. Seth, or this new path, would overcome the path of his brother Cain. Since Cain represents the path of selfishness, it would be reasonable to say that the path of Seth is one of selflessness.

Spirit-man was created in the image of God and is destined to express and demonstrate spiritual perfection. In the universe, including all of God's creation is set a balancing power of good which causes a readjustment to bring everything back into harmony. Any transgression of the law, any wandering away from that which is wholesome (holy) and true must be brought into order.

Cain went to the Land of Nod, a place where the mind wanders in uncertainty. A place of bewilderment or feelings of perplexity and confusion. This condition is commonly referred to as 'sleep,' or a state of being in the dark. It is this state or condition that one needs to 'awaken' from.

Remember, therefore, what you have received and heard; obey it, and repent. But if you do not wake up, I will come like a thief, and you will not know at what time I will come to you. Revelation 3:3

Like Cain, man has wandered away from that which is wholesome and true. This is why man is constantly searching for the truth, but truth is hard to find in the dark. As Jesus says the Christ may come to you but if you are asleep, you won't even know it.

As seen in the characters of the Bible when man drifts away from Spirit a reaction sets in that draws him back to a reasonable, sensible, and saner level. Thus, man evolves, grows, and finally comes to fuller understanding of his perfect good. Man's growth into the Christ Consciousness is accelerated as he comes into knowledge of Truth, and it is this knowledge of Truth that makes him free. As he becomes more and more awake, he becomes more in harmony with the Christ Consciousness and in harmony with his true spiritual self.

When man comes to the end of the road (pigpen) he begins to look to a higher source of meaning in his wasted life and realizes the futility of his human efforts to better himself. Seth had a son whom he named Enosh (Heb), *a miserable man, mortal man.* Apart from Spirit, man is miserable, and his mortality calls on the name of the Lord.

Everyone who calls on the name of the Lord will be saved. Joel 2:32

The Conscience

Conscience – *The inherent ability of every healthy human being to perceive what is right and what is wrong, and on the strength of this perception, to control, monitor, evaluate and execute their actions.*

To counter act selfishness and to bring man back in harmony with the Truth a new form of consciousness was introduced. This new consciousness is called 'conscience,' or an inner feeling or voice viewed as action and guide to right-mindedness away from one's wrong-mindedness or bad or evil behavior. Seth began the line of religious traditions and rituals that would keep God in the mind of man, and perhaps make him feel guilty about his wrong mindedness. Without it man would remain asleep wandering in the land of uncertainty. Without a conscience (Seth) man is unguided, without direction, without guidance alone ravished with fear, agitated with apprehension, and banished to exile from his source life. Death is his future.

A period of time is needed for the new states of consciousness to develop in the earth plane. We see this evolvement in the stories of the Bible. Genesis to Noah is the development of Spirit. From Noah to Moses is the development of the body-mind. From Moses to Jesus is the development of the mind or the mental. We see this in Jesus' selection of his twelve disciples. Each disciple represents a faculty of the mind. For example, Peter – faith and John – love. It is these faculties of mind (Abel) that control our animalistic behavior.

The sons of Jacob (12 tribes of Israel), also represent the faculty of mind in this case the body-mind. For example, Joseph (11th son) – the state of consciousness in which we increase in character. Judah (4th son) – the spiritual faculty that corresponds to accumulation or increase in the mental. The body may respond to the mind but as Paul says first comes the natural man then the spiritual man.

If there is a natural body, there is also a spiritual body. So, it is written: "The first man Adam became a living being"; the last Adam, a life-giving spirit. The spiritual did not come first, but the natural, and after that the spiritual. 1 Corinthians 15:44-46

The Apostle Paul of course here is speaking of the progression of Spirit in the earth plane. The thought-forms came from Spirit, they became the Natural-man, then the Natural-man returns to Spirit.

The Apostle Paul goes on to say,

The first man was of the dust of the earth, the second man from heaven, so also are those who are of heaven. And just as we have borne the likeness of the earthly man, so shall we [so let us] bear the likeness of the man from heaven. 1 Corinthians 15:47-49

The consciousness of the Natural-man is of the Earth and remains in the Earth (from dust to dust). Spirit-man is the spiritual consciousness; he came from heaven and will soon return.

The Wilderness steps are a part of the mental development. Remember the wilderness represent uncultivated and undisciplined thought in individual consciousness. To restore order and harmony a reaction and adjustment is needed. To restore order a system or government (Ten Commandments) was established to exercise authority over that which was unrulily and out of control. That which was out of control was selfishness.

Before the Law of Moses, sin may have existed, but without a law or system of rules to define correct behavior and punishments to regulate man's actions, sin was never considered wrong and probably why these laws were not easily accepted.

Therefore, just as sin entered the world through one man, and death through sin, and in this way, death came to all men, because all sinned – for before the law was given, sin was in the world. But sin is not taken into account when there is no law. Romans 5:12-13

The Laws were not the only commands given at this time; there were also rules and regulations regarding Hebrew servants, personal injury, protection of property, social responsibilities, laws of justice and mercy, Sabbath laws, annual festivals, and the establishment of the Tabernacle.

All of these laws and rules were meant to become part of the conscience. As laws and rules, they served as guides to what was considered sin in the eyes of God. Without punishment for the crimes against God, the laws would have no effect. This is likely where the concept of the law of cause and effect originated. Every action now, whether good or bad, would have consequences depending on the intention or spirit behind the action. This is why the Old Testament focuses on punishment. It is primarily about the actions of the body, which responds to its environment. Punishment involves pain, something the body-mind understands and responds to.

Many don't believe in reincarnation, but it is necessary for man to make sense of his actions. If we only have one experience, whether good or bad, we don't experience the opposite and therefore never fully understand the Truth. Remember, the Earth is the plane of blind experimentation, and we need to experiment with both good and bad to understand the difference between the two no matter how many life times it takes.

The Tabernacle

Along with the Ten Commandments and the laws and ordinances that Moses received at this time, he was also given the perfect pattern for the Tabernacle of worship for the living God. The Tabernacle represents the body-temporal or the temporary body that comes before the regenerated permanent body, as represented by king Solomon's temple built in Jerusalem. In the wilderness, God is worshipped in a tent, symbolizing a transitory state of mind. This is the perishable body.

The Old Testament is about the evolution of the body of man. Every facet of the Tabernacle has a spiritual, mental, and physical relationship to the body. In the Tabernacle, we find all the furnishings that will later be used to build the great Temple: the altar, laver, candlestick, and the Ark of the Covenant. All the utensils were made of gold, silver, or precious wood.

The pattern given to Moses for the construction of the Tabernacle represents a pattern of the individual entity (body) and the place where man meets his Maker. Each of the twelve tribes of Israel was to follow all the directions and details outlined in Exodus 25-40. Cooperation between the tribes was necessary because all twelve tribes were involved in its construction. Psychologically, the construction of the Tabernacle demanded that they recognize a state of perfection.

The directions for the completed Tabernacle are both symbolic and literal. The outer structure was made of flimsy material or cloth, just as the fleshy covering of the body is also flimsy and perishable. However, when God instructed Moses to build the temporary dwelling, it came with the promise of a more permanent dwelling to come. Thus, the body of man, even the body of Christ, is a promise of a more imperishable one.

The Tabernacle establishes a new state of consciousness. Although we build our own mind and character, it is God who furnishes the design to be built. The intricate anatomy of our physical bodies represents a reflection of a spiritual pattern, which we can find within ourselves. The symbolic relationship between the mind, body, and soul and the Tabernacle are as follows:

- Outer Court (the body)
- Inner Court or Holy Place (the mind)
- Holy of Holies (the soul or Spirit)

The Tabernacle is a unified service of the body-mind, the body-physical, the body-spiritual; or that vehicle that is without nails (as was the Tabernacle as a pattern), not bound together, yet a covering, a place, an understanding for a unified activity with Creative Forces, or the power of God. The veil without, the holy within, as in the holy of holies.

Before the High Priest could enter, he was to be consecrated (declared sacred), he must be washed (cleansed outward-body) and he must be purified (cleansed inward-mind). Before Moses and the people could face the Passover, they had to cleanse their bodies and minds. Also, before approaching the

Mountain, they had to cleanse themselves for three days and purify their minds. This is part of The Godward Steps, to cleanse our bodies and our minds of falsehood before we enter the Holy of Holies.

The first step of the building of the Tabernacle was the giving of the gifts of jewelry, gold, silver, brass, spices, oils, skins, linens, and acacia wood to be used in its construction (Exodus 25:1-9). These gifts had to be willingly given from the heart of the individual (Exodus 25:2). To build the spiritual body, we first must give up our material ideas. The 'Temple' is the inheritance of those who are faithful. Faith must become substance.

The Power of Three

The Tabernacle consisted of three main parts:

1. The Alter of Sacrifice
2. The Holy Place
3. The Holy of Holies

The Holy Place contained the Table for the Bread of Presence, the Golden Lampstand, and the Altar of Incense. The Holy of Holies contained the Ark of the Covenant, a sacred chest which was a symbol of God's Divine Presence. A curtain or veil, made of costly material, divided the two main sections.

The expressions as shown in the Tabernacle and the orders as given for its construction —such as the size, the shape, the measurements, the figures above the Holy of Holies, specified colors for the hangings, the manner in which each board was to be set, and how each skin was to be used or dyed – serve as a symbol of aspects within ourselves. Hence, these material objects become symbolic in the experience and application of those in worship. They became living symbols in the experience of the individual.

Much of the symbolism in the book of Revelation is based on Old Testament experiences. Many Old Testament patterns and symbols relate to the forces within the perfect structure of the Temple of Man.

Cherubim

Place the cover on top of the ark and put in the ark the Testimony, which I shall give you. There, above the cover between the two cherubim that are over the ark of the Testimony, I will meet with you and give you all my commands for the Israelites. Exodus 25:21-22

The two cherubim (winged celestial beings) have strategic positions in the place of communication. Perhaps these two angels have the same metaphysical significance as the two witnesses in Revelation 11:3. The spiritual-mental (Super-Consciousness), and the physical-mental are likely represented by the two cherubim above the mercy seat.

The Veil

Make the tabernacle with ten curtains of finely twisted linen and blue and purple and scarlet yarn, with cherubim worked into them by a skilled craftsman. Exodus 26:1

If these curtains represent the ten senses of man, then the veils are an appropriate symbol. This shows the sense-man, or the natural man is still 'behind the veil'. It was this heavy curtain in the Temple at Jerusalem that was torn in half at the time of Jesus' death during his crucifixion (Matthew 27:51).

It is the veil of sense thoughts that conceals the spiritual body from the natural man. The tearing of the veil is the last step in the regeneration of the natural man as he gives up the perishable body for the imperishable and eternal body.

It was at that moment when the veil was torn that Jesus passed from the Natural-man back to Spirit-man.

And when Jesus had cried out again in a loud voice, he gave up his spirit. At that moment the curtain of the temple was torn in two from top to bottom. The earth shook and the rocks split. The tombs broke open and the bodies of many holy people who had died were raised to life. They came out of the tombs, and after Jesus' resurrection they went into the holy city and appeared to many people. Matthew 27:50-52

It appears that those holy who had died were also included in the resurrection. But it wasn't until Jesus had undone the error of Adam that this was possible. Think about that for a moment.

The Mercy Seat

And you shall make a mercy seat of pure gold, two and a half cubits long, and a cubit and a half breadth. And you shall make two cherubim of gold of cast work shall you make them on the two sides of the mercy seat. Exodus 25:17-18

The mercy seat was a symbol to help the people understand what they were to expect of God. They didn't understand it then, and too often we don't today. God is Love, and in His Love is kindness, patience, and understanding.

We will never know the meaning of mercy until we understand God's mercy to us. The best means of obtaining this awareness is to practice showing mercy to others. Remember it has to be within us before it is outwardly recognized.

To have our bodies and minds conform to the same pattern as the Tabernacle it is necessary to do certain things uniformly and with the proper attention to detail. But not so ritualistic as to forget the spirit or purpose behind the rite. The daily ritual should remind us of the necessity to make our lives in accord with our spiritual purposes. We should dedicate part of our day to meditation, entering into the Holy of Holies within ourselves. We must prepare ourselves for this communion with the highest forces known. It is essential to make a habit of daily activities that remind us that the body is the temple where God has promised to speak with us.

When seeking to find the answers, don't look only outward but open the door to your consciousness and embrace the promises that are sure in Him. You will find that just as the pattern that was shown to Moses on the mount and as Jesus faced great temptations in the wilderness as the Christ Consciousness is lifted up, draws all men and women unto God.

Stay close to God's covenant, and don't be swayed by the advice of others. Instead, turn inward, knowing that the POWER lies there. Entering the Holy of Holies within ourselves is where we will find STRENGTH that surpasses man's physical abilities.

Aaron's Breastplate

Whenever Aaron enters the Holy Place, he will bear the name of the sons of Israel over his heart on the breast-piece of decision as a continuing memorial before the Lord. Exodus 28:29

Each of the twelve precious stones in Aaron's breastplate carried the vibration of the tribe it represented. The messages from God of each tribe were interpreted by Aaron according to his understanding of the emanations from the stones.

God knows every soul by name. What name? All the many lives and names the entity has used during their material experience in the earthly plane. Hence, every name is relative to that which is accomplished by the soul in its sojourn throughout its whole experience Godward. Our name carries a vibration, and the sum of that vibration is how near we are to the Creative Force itself. The higher the vibration, the closer we are to God. This is why it is said that Jesus' name is above all names as he has reached the highest of vibrations and is the one closes to God.

Each soul has a definite influence on the experiences it may undergo. This influence is evident in organizations and even religious associations. When you have set a vibration through the activity of the soul force, you are either in parallel (the plain), in direct accord (the mountain), or in opposition (the city) to constructive force –whatever may be the position or activity of the soul in infinity. For we are gods! But are we becoming devil's or real gods?

Each color also has a vibration and meaning to the consciousness. Red represents anger but a variation of the color such as rosy to most means delight and joy. Stones, minerals, or colors may be used when meditating or to find attunement, but these do not give the message. They only attune oneself so that the Christ Consciousness may give the message. DO NOT listen to a message of a stone, a number or even of a star (Zodiac) for they are but servants of the Lord and Master of all just as we are masters of our own destiny.

In Babylonian mythology, certain gods were messengers to mankind, and wore upon their breasts "Tablets of Destiny." Through these stones, the people could inquire of their gods for yes and no answers to questions concerning their destiny as a nation and the fate of their kings. This is an interesting parallel with the Israelites. Aaron, as high priest and the spokesman for Jehovah, breastplate was used exclusively in matters concerning the king or nation. Perhaps, in earlier days, the use of stones to attune to a higher consciousness was very common.

Each element, each stone, each variation of stone, has its own atomic movement, held together by the units of energy that in the universe are concentrated in that particular activity. Hence, they come under varied activities according to their color, vibration, or emanation.

Urim and Thummim

Urim and Thummim (Exodus 28:29-30), were two mysterious objects used by the high priest to receive messages from God. They have been interpreted in a variety of ways, from 'purity and perfection' to 'revelation and truth'. Certainly, the high priest had to strive for purity and perfection in his heart to receive a revelation of truth. This applies to each of us as well. The true importance of Urim and Thummim is that they were aides through which the priest could attune his consciousness to the Divine.

Strange Fire

And there went out fire from before the Lord and devoured them and they died before the Lord. Leviticus 10:2

The force in nature known as electricity is that same creative force of God in action. Free-will, which is as powerful as electricity, can be a force for either evil or good, depending on how we use it. Through their knowledge of the Godhead and its energies, and the vibrations they raised in worship and devotion, the Hebrews could electrify a mountain, part the sea, or make water spring from a stone. Misuse of this tremendous force resulted in death, as it did for Nadab and Abihu.

Nadad and Abihu were the first two sons of Aaron the priest (Exodus 6:23). Contrary to God's commands, the two sons of Aaron took their censers, put fire in them, and added incense; and they offered unauthorized fire before God. So, fire came out from the presence of the Lord and consumed them.

Many people lose sight of their purpose, and their ideals, and have presented strange fires upon the alters of truth leading to their destruction and sadly the destruction of others. So long as there is perfect coordination in self, in the physical body, in the mental-body, in the spiritual-body all things work together for the good. When there is rebellion between the mind, body, and spirit then there is disconnection, destruction, disconcerted effort, and things go awry. The mind, body, and spirit are to be as one or else death in the physical ensues, by the disconcerted action and in coordinated action of the mental, physical, and spiritual.

Awry is away from the appropriate, planned, or expected course. We should present ourselves as God has planned and not tell God how to do His work. Rather we should be a channel of blessing through which others may be given an opportunity to approach His throne. We should not cast our pearls (truths) before swine or conduct ourselves in a manner that our good is seen as evil or our evil is seen as good. Study to show thyself approved unto God, avoiding the appearances of evil, knowing that our actions are a reflection of who or what we serve whether that be fame, fortune, power, position, or God.

In rabbinical literature, two opposing views are taken concerning Nadad and Abihu. One view is that the brothers were inventive and or creative in their efforts to bring Divine Fire into the congregation. The other view, which is probably the case, is that the brothers were consumed by their own selfishness. They considered themselves superior to Moses and Aaron and were jealous of their leadership. They also felt they were too good to be married. Remember selfishness leads to Spiritual Destruction, Starvation (pigpen) and possible death.

STEP 13

Rebellion | Depravity

Rebellion – *The action or process of resisting authority, control, or convention.*

Depravity – *Moral corruption or wickedness.*

The Golden Calf

"Come make us gods [or a god] who will go before us. As for this fellow Moses who brought us up out of Egypt, we don't know what has happened to him." Exodus 32:1

Up until this point in your journey Godward it has been all about your body, its cravings, its desires, and its senses. Now that these cravings and desires are subsiding, and the sense consciousness is not being fed, all the memories of the flesh (Egypt) are starting to creep back into your mind.

During Moses' absence, the Israelites took off all their gold jewelry along with all the other gold trinkets they brought with them out of Egypt and gave them to Aaron who cast them into the shape of a calf for the people to worship.

He took what they handed him and made it into an idol cast in the shape of a calf, fashioning it with a tool. Then they said, "These are your gods [or this is your god], O 'Israel, who brought you up out of Egypt." Exodus 32:4

Whatever selfishness remains in you will rise to the surface, and all the pieces that are left will manifest into one large idol of worship. Whatever you still value and whatever you selfishly possess will become your idol of worship because you have been holding on to its memory. This doesn't necessarily have to be gold and jewelry; it can be anything you are afraid to let go of. It could be someone you're involved with, a job, a car, sex, pornography, alcohol, cigarettes, or anything that feeds the senses. But whatever it is, it will manifest in your life. The hardest of these to overcome is some past sexual relationship. For me, this encounter was short-lived, and I hope it will be for you as well. I realized that I no longer needed this person and that there was no way I was going to let them entice me back into the world. My abstaining from sex for five years was probably to prepare me for this temptation.

Aaron (Heb.) means *illumined* and *enlightener.* Metaphysically Aaron is the Executive Power of divine law. Aaron was the first priest of Israel and the bearer of intellectual light to the Israelites. Aaron signifies the ruling intellectual consciousness.

Aaron's casting of the *'golden calf'* signifies the false states of thought or idols, that man builds into his consciousness when he perceives the Truth but doesn't carry his spiritual ideals into execution. The Israelites admittedly believed some spiritual entity had brought them out of Egypt, however, they hadn't seen this entity for themselves but was seen through Moses. When Moses stayed too long on the mountain, they no longer felt the presence of that entity. They needed something else physical that would give them that feeling.

As they said, *"This is your god, O 'Israel, who brought you up out of Egypt."*

Like the Israelites, you are not yet ready to realize that it was your own power that brought you out of the world. Just like the Israelites, you have chosen to let your thoughts function on a lower plane of consciousness.

In God's anger, He told Moses that because of the actions of the people, He would destroy them. Moses persuaded God not to destroy the people and let him deal with them. Moses brought the Ten Commandments down the mountain with him, and when he saw the people dancing and singing around the golden idol, he threw the tablets from his hands, breaking them into pieces. In his anger, Moses tells those whoever is for the Lord to rally around him. The Levites came to his side. Then Moses told each Levite man to grab a sword and go through the camp and kill everyone who was not with them. They killed over three thousand.

The Israelites in the wilderness symbolize the illuminated thoughts in consciousness undergoing spiritual discipline. They collectively represent our religious thoughts. As we journey from Egypt to the Promised Land, our spiritual consciousness, and religious thoughts (Israelites) begin to awaken to Spiritual Truth. These religious thoughts pertain to the real and enduring ideas upon which man and the universe are founded. They are always endeavoring to follow the inner leading of the Divine Law.

The purpose of these spiritual thoughts in the body (children of Israel down in Egypt) is to raise the body-mind up gradually to a more enduring life. When we affirm the Truth and yearn for our release from material bondage a couple of things happen:

1. Our Pharaoh-ego, the ruler of our body consciousness, does not want to let go of its position of power.

2. Our Moses-ego begins the process of drawing us out of our slavery to the flesh and demands that Pharaoh let our spiritual thoughts (Israelites) go.

This condition, known as *"the hardening of hearts,"* occurs when our spiritual thoughts are not freed unless Pharaoh hardens his heart or his heart is caused to be hardened. You may feel, during this period of letting go, either by your own choice or through the actions of those around you, that you have failed somehow and now seek to restore what you've lost. However, in reality, you haven't lost anything; in fact, you may find that what you have set in motion will gradually make you stronger and more spiritual. Previously, you may have had spiritual thoughts, but over time, they have been obscured by physical and material conditions.

The strength of the Israelites lay in their faith in God. Have faith that your spiritual thoughts know the Truth and strive to follow it. The disciples of Christ Jesus were instructed to go first to the lost sheep of the house of Israel (obscured spiritual thoughts) because those thoughts of the knowledge of Truth are the first to be redeemed. Then, next to the Gentiles, or our worldly thoughts, external thoughts that function through the senses. Once you have developed the power of your spiritual thoughts, you will be able to redeem your sense-driven thoughts (Gentiles).

I am not ashamed of the gospel, because it is the power of God for the salvation of everyone who believes, first for the Jew, then for the Gentile. For in the gospel a righteousness from God is revealed, a righteousness that is by faith from first [or is faith to faith] just as it is written: "The righteous will live by faith" (Habakkuk 2:4) Romans 1:16-17

The Mountain of Solitude

After smashing the Ten Commandments in anger, Moses went up the mountain again to get another set of tablets. This ascent into the mountain to receive the Divine Law symbolizes the elevated, exalted state of mind that we must attain before we can receive spiritual inspiration. To cultivate our spiritual growth, we must undertake daily pilgrimages to the mountain of solitude, achieved through silence and meditation. However, we mustn't linger too long on the mountaintop and neglect the lower thoughts below. If we do, our lower thoughts will seek alternative sources of inspiration that deviate from the Truth. This is illustrated by the making of the golden calf by Aaron, the high priest, who represents our intellectual consciousness.

When our intellect becomes the center of our consciousness all our precious thoughts (gold & jewels) are poured into it resulting in many material structures (golden calves), that are built up and worshipped. Many believe that money is the answer to all their problems. Many believe that if they had money, they could do a lot of good. This is worshipping the golden calf – making material things greater than spiritual things. This idea must be ground to powder as Moses did to the golden calf before the true method is put into action.

God is sufficient, and if we are willing to obey His law, a way will open, and all our plans will proceed in the right way. Money will come to us as our servant, not as our master. Those who prioritize acquiring wealth before doing the Lord's work are essentially worshipping the golden calf. They doubt that God will provide.

The Lord's work has always been done by those who are willing to serve. There is a long line of servants, such as Jesus and Paul whose only capital was the Spirit of God.

But he said to me, "My grace is sufficient for you, for my power is made perfect in weakness." Therefore, I will boast all the more gladly about my weakness, so that Christ's power may rest on me. This is why, for Christ's sake, I delight in weaknesses, in insults, in hardships in persecution, in difficulties. For when I am weak, then I am strong. 2 Corinthians 12:9-10

You may feel that you are losing your strength by losing the world and your ego. But what you lose in material you will gain ten times in Spirit, and it is Spirit that gives us life. The world only takes it away.

Jesus said, "Whoever has found the world and become rich should renounce the world. The Gospel of Thomas v.110

The Enemies of God

Whenever the ark set out, Moses said, "Rise up, O Lord! May your enemies be scattered; may your foes flee before you." Numbers 10:35

If we do what's right in our heart and do right in self then know that we have no enemies, and what is ours cannot be taken from us. Those who try such are enemies to themselves. Don't look at them as your enemy but feel sorry for them for they have misinterpreted what is right. They are the ones who are wrong. They are the ones who are wrong-minded.

Moses prayed that God's enemies be scattered, not his own. The Bible gives no indication of who the enemies were. Was it an external enemy or was it his own people who bore a spirit of enmity with God's? Shortly after this prayer, several more rebellions occur. One of the issues was about meat (Numbers 11). In another, a personal issue was provoked by Miriam and Aaron, Moses' own brother and sister, over Moses' marriage to an Ethiopian.

The Spies

The Lord said to Moses, "Send some men to explore the land of Caanan, which I am giving to the Israelites. From each ancestral tribe send one of its leaders." Numbers 13:12

After a three-day journey, Moses was told to select individuals in whom all Israel had confidence to spy out the Promised Land. After forty days, they returned, bringing fruit from the land and delivering a positive report. However, they also reported sighting giants and fortified cities.

The giants were most likely descendants of the Nephilim, remnants of those beings who had entered into materiality outside the line of Adam. The Nephilim were the fearsome offspring of the sons of God and the daughters of men, who were said to have been destroyed by the great flood in the days of Noah.

Those thought-forms or children of God who thought projected their form in the earth plane and entangled themselves in the animal kingdom, over time their thought bodies gradually took form. These took on many sizes as to stature, from that as may be called the midget to the giants.

Scripture states that there were giants on the Earth in those days (Genesis 6:4), men as tall as what would be termed today ten or twelve feet in stature, and in proportion. Most of these creatures were destroyed in the great flood but some apparently survived and now were living in the Promised Land.

If this is true, then we can understand why this line needed to be destroyed, and why Joshua, Moses' aide, had the responsibility to do so. Once they were slain, and their race extinguished, they would reincarnate through those channels that were the result of the creation of Adam. Their souls then could begin the upward process of evolution Godward.

God had promised that the children of Israel would possess the Holy Land and that all of these tribes would be destroyed. Now they were being tested as to whether God's promises were true.

But the men who went up with him said, "We can't attack those people; they are stronger than we are. And they spread among the Israelites a bad report about the land they had explored. They said, "The land we explored devours those living in it. All the people we saw there are of great size. We saw the Nephilim there (the descendants of Anak come from the Nephilim). We seemed like grasshoppers in our own eyes, and we looked the same to them." Numbers 13:31-33

We must gain confidence in ourselves by having trust in the promises of God. By doing so, we can make amends for many of our shortcomings in this life as well as past lives. By doing what's right and aligning with the divine within us, we tap into the Creative Force. If we attune our self, the ego, the I AM, to the divine, there is nothing that will keep us from achieving any position of power we desire. However, if our desires become selfish, we are headed to the pigpen and possible death.

In Atlantis, the Children of the Law of One joined with the Sons of Belial (children of darkness) and brought sin, destruction, and death. Some turned away from the teachings of love, kindness, and patience to gratify selfish desires, rejecting all the warnings given by those spokesmen from the holy sources and the keepers of the Law of One. Their selfishness eventually led to the destruction of Atlantis. By supporting Caleb and Joshua in their favorable report of the Promised Land and uniting with those who were convinced by the Holy Spirit, the opportunity was made to correct those weaknesses which began in Atlantis.

Remember what has been done in error must be undone. If we turn from the way of truth to gratify self's desires and vanities, woe be unto the entity, not only here in this life, but in those experiences to come.

The Wilderness Purpose

In the wilderness with Moses were those who were the reincarnation of the Sons of God who had entered the earth plane in the beginning with Amilius, the leader of Atlantis, but had fallen away from their spiritual purpose. The Wilderness period gave them, as it does all of us, the opportunity to re-establish our relationship with God, which we can either accept or reject.

That night all the people of the community raised their voice and wept aloud. All the Israelites grumbled against Moses and Aaron, and the whole assembly said to them, "If only we had died in Egypt! Or in this desert! Why is the Lord bringing us to this land only to let us fall by the sword? Our wives and children will be taken as plunder. Wouldn't it be better for us to go back to Egypt?" And they said to each other, "We should choose a leader and go back to Egypt." Numbers 14:1-3

For two years the children of Israel had been listening to Moses and Aaron preach. They were given the commandments of God under which they were to live. As slaves in Egypt, they were used to having their taskmasters make decisions for them. Now they were forced to make their own decisions. If they had listened to what God had promised and kept their faith in Him, they would have found the courage to face their adversaries, subdued their enemies, and taken possession of the Promised Land. But the fear of capture overcame them, so they rebelled again, against Moses and God. Thus, a long period of wandering began.

You have the same opportunity here as did the Children of Promise. It's time to stop listening to your taskmasters and start making decisions for yourself. Trust in God and know His promises are true. Reentering the world (The Land of Canaan) may be scary but you can't go back to Egypt and remaining in the wilderness will only lead to death.

Korah's Rebellion

Throughout the wilderness period, Moses was plagued by one rebellion after another. The people complained when they had no food to eat and complained when they had no water to drink. Even Aaron and Miriam (older sister of Moses and Aaron) rebelled when Moses married an Ethiopian woman. Still, other rebellions occurred when factions, such as Korah's began to question Moses' authority and his right to be their leader.

Korah, the son of Izhar, the son of Kohath, the son of Levi, and certain Reubenites – Dathan and Abiram, the sons of Eliab, and On son of Peleth, all started a faction and they rose up before Moses with other rebellious members of the community along with two hundred and fifty chiefs of the assembly, who at that time were men of renown.

They came as a group to oppose Moses and Aaron and said to them, "You have gone too far! The whole community is holy, every one of them. Why then do you set yourselves above the Lord's assembly." Numbers 16:3

The leaders of the uprising, Korah, Dathan, and Abiram, represent rebellious thoughts in our mind.

- Korah – Coldness and unproductiveness of life and good.

- Dathan – A leading thought in the religious consciousness of man that is established in the letter of the law as being the fount, or spring – the source, cause, or motive of religious service and Truth.

- Abiram – Arrogance of pride or the nobility of true spiritual exaltation. Presumptuous, arrogant, and rebellious thoughts or tendencies that are caused by <u>spiritual pride</u>.

This is seen as a period of condemning others, and a pattern of withdrawal, unbelief, and unfaithfulness. This period of rebellion can cause further suffering mentally and the trying of your patience as by fire. Further wanderings and tribulations are sure to follow if the rebellion is not put down.

On more than one occasion Moses's authority was questioned. Even after the miracles they had seen him perform, the people disputed whether God had really chosen him or not.

When Moses heard this, he fell facedown. Then he said, "In the morning the Lord will show who belongs to him and who is holy, and he will have that person come near him. The man he chooses he will cause to come near him. You, Korah, and all your followers are to do this: Take censers and tomorrow put fire and incense in them before the Lord. The man the Lord chooses will be the one who is holy. You Levites have gone too far!" Numbers 16:4-7

We must constantly make tests within ourselves as to which is God's way or our way. As long as we are not fully convinced by the Spirit, there is always the possibility of being deceived by others, or our own egos. But if we truly are sincere, we can bring it all before God, and the results of this testing will show us the true path, pattern, or leader to follow. It should be within us to analyze ourselves, and constantly search for the answers within. For the ego is always there waiting to raise its ugly head.

You might assume that if the Israelites had walked across the Red Sea on dry land, they would never would have forgotten it. But all too often, we vow to ourselves only to forget them before the sun sets. We read these stories in the Bible and believe they belong to a distant past, thinking we are much more advanced today, but in many ways, we are still the same. They were selfish then, and we are selfish now. That much hasn't changed.

Sometimes we hold to our duty to others or to those whom we love. Yet this can bring destructive experiences in our lives. Although we may gain from an experience at first, later it brings resentment. Therefore, it is necessary in the present time to hold to the TRUTH of the spiritual life and spiritual processes as related to the material and mental forces. We must always return to a physical, mental, and spiritual understanding in order for there to be a normal balance.

Always seek the truth regarding those in positions of authority. Recognize any shady dealings among those around you and take the upper hand when dealing with weaknesses in character or nature displayed by your friends or associates. DO NOT BE TEMPTED BY THEM. Always remain true to yourself, and you will always be true to others.

Then the Lord said to Moses, "Say to the assembly, 'Move away from the tents of Korah, Dathan and Abiram.' Moses got up and went to

Dathan and Abiram, and the elders of Israel followed him. He warned the assembly, "Move back from the tents of these wicked men! Do not touch anything belonging to them, or you will be swept away because of all their sins." ... Korah, Dathan, and Abriam had come out and were standing with their wives, children, and little ones at the entrances of their tents. Then Moses said, "This is how you will know that the Lord has sent me to do all these things and that it was not my idea. If these men die a natural death and experience only what usually happens to men, then the Lord has not sent me. But if the Lord brings about something totally new, and the earth opens its mouth and swallows them, with everything that belongs to them, and they go down alive into the grave [sheol], then you will know that these men have treated the Lord with contempt." Numbers 23-30

As soon as Moses finished speaking the ground split apart and the earth opened up and swallowed them and all their possessions.

As we continue The Wilderness Steps, it is important to remain true to what we have learned and experienced thus far. If we turn to pursuits that are solely for selfish gain (offer strange fire), those pursuits will become detestable in our earthly experiences and will ultimately be consumed by those same experiences. We can easily lose all that we have gained during our time in the wilderness. Troubles will arise if we strive for greater status or seek to advance our selfish interests through position and power. Self-aggrandizement brings only defiance to the lessons and tenets (fundamental principles) and applications of extremes in a material world.

They went down alive into the grave [sheol], with everything they owned; the earth closed over them, and they perished and were gone from the community. At their cries, all the Israelites around them fled, shouting, "The earth is going to swallow us too!" And fire came out from the Lord and consumed the 250 men who were offering the incense. Numbers 16:33-35

The people were destroyed because they allied themselves with those who rebelled against Aaron and Moses. Their downfall was not due to defying God, but rather defying their spiritual leaders. This raises the question: should the sincerity of individuals or groups always be the measure of the final outcome of a situation? Scripture teaches that how you judge others is how you will also be judged whether for good or bad. This is a universal law.

"Do not judge, or you too will be judged. For in the same way you judge others, you will be judged, and with the measure you use, it will be measured to you..." Matthew 7:1-2

The law is a universal consciousness and can be applied in the experiences of everyone who seeks the truth in their relationship to the Creative Forces, or God. The Creative Force is an influence within and without, and answers by the way we apply that Creative Influence in our relationships with others.

How we meet our brothers, or to say how we interact with them, and by what measure or degree we treat them, good or bad, that same measure or degree we also will have to meet. In this life or the next. No one is above the law.

As we stand for the Truth, removing false beliefs and errors from our minds, and dedicate ourselves to serving others, we can bring peace out of arguments and quarrels. We can halt contentious activities that may escalate into mob-like behavior and gain the ability to counsel those who are individually sad and abused.

Desire is fire, and it purifies. If we create a desire to be at-one with God, eventually we will achieve the object of our desire – peace, unity, and happiness.

Meribah

Meribah (Heb.), *pleading; contention; strife; quarrel,* was a place in the wilderness the Israelites came to where there was no water.

Now there was no water for the community, and the people gathered in opposition to Moses and Aaron. They quarreled with Moses and said, "If only we had died when our brothers fell dead before the Lord! ..." "Why did you bring the Lord's community into this desert, that we and our livestock should die here? Numbers 20:2-3

You may be asking yourself the same questions! "Why did I ever start these steps and why did I ever leave my old life?" "It wasn't the best life but at least I had one!" Don't think that I didn't ask the same question.

It seems like every time we have an opportunity to overcome the sins or errors in our lives and finally prove that God's promises are true, we find a reason to murmur, complain, and doubt God. As long as everything is going well in our life, we are happy and feel our faith in God is strong but when things go awry, we start questioning God and our faith. Don't feel like you are the only one who felt this way I too during my wilderness journey murmured and complained.

"Watch and pray so that you will not fall into temptation. The spirit is willing, but the flesh is weak." Matthew 26:41

Remember what it is that you are battling at this point in your journey – the flesh. The desires of the flesh must first be overcome before we can venture into the Promised Land and deal with the desires of the mind. If our selfishness is not eliminated it will follow us to the mental development of our journey – The Promised Land Steps. Selfishness of the body-mind is one thing, but selfishness mentally is another. The mind can control the body but if the mind is selfish, it is out of control. It cannot subdue and have dominion over our selfish actions. It will only lead to more.

When they needed water, they blamed Moses instead of turning to God for guidance and direction. Each time Pharaoh refused to let the people go, Moses didn't doubt what God had already told him. He went back and asked God what he should do next. If his people had followed Moses' example, things would have been much different.

The tendency to murmur and complain will slowly dimmish as we progress Godward, in Spirit and in Truth. Once we replace the "old man" with the "new man" (the Christ), the urge to complain will cease. You will finally realize that there really is nothing to complain about. We have everything that we could possibly need. Complaining is just another sign of fear. Remember fear is a state of mind that we have created for ourselves.

So Moses took the staff from the Lord's presence, just as he commanded him. He and Aaron gathered the assembly together in front of the rock and Moses said to them, "Listen, you rebels, must we bring you water out of this rock?" Then Moses raised his arm and struck the rock twice with his staff. Water gushed out, and the community and their livestock drank. Numbers 20:10-11

Be cautious here; remember, we are dealing with the Moses-ego, not the True-ego. Moses must have felt superior to the community, as most egos do, feeling superior to others. This is one of the hardest lessons you will have to learn – humbleness of spirit, especially if one, like Moses, is in a position of authority and power. Because Moses didn't give glory to God for bringing forth the water from the rock look at what God had to say to Moses.

But the Lord said to Moses and Aaron, "Because you did not trust in me enough to honor me as holy in the sight of the Israelites, you will not bring this community into the land I give them." Numbers 20:12

As we draw closer to the Promised Land, we increasingly rely on the God within to guide us. Our Moses-ego may begin to dominate, and a new ego will emerge. This spiritual ego can be as destructive and defiant as the Pharaoh-ego. The new emerging ego may cease seeking wisdom from God and instead rely on itself. We observe this pattern in certain religious leaders, and it is becoming more common. These are the self-righteous.

At this point, you will likely be tired of all the emotions and murmuring. The quarrel between the conscious (physical) and the subconscious (spiritual) will feel like a broken record, endlessly repeating the same emotions. The time has come to relinquish the egoism of self. After all, the Moses-ego and the Pharaoh-ego are one and the same - YOU. They represent two sides of the same coin – the physical and the spiritual. Although they may seem separate, both are part of the whole – the body. If these two egos are not resolved, the wandering in the wilderness will persist until one emerges victorious.

It was because of their doubt and complaints and the emerging ego of superiority that caused the children of Israel to die in the wilderness. No one over the age of 20, other than Jacob and Caleb, made it to the Promised Land. Even Moses and Aaron died in the wilderness.

What you must admit to yourself is that there is no going back to Egypt, the flesh, and the old lifestyle. In addition, the Pharaoh-ego and the Moses-ego have no place in the Promised Land. Both selfish egos must be left on the wilderness side of the Jordan River. If the murmuring and quarreling continue, it may mean certain death as it did for those who were wandering in the wilderness.

We must be of service to mankind and not just to appear that way. Murmuring, complaining, doubt, and fear show that we are not trusting in God. If we are not trusting and have faith in God as we say we do, then we are of no service to others.

"The most important one," answered Jesus, "is this: 'Hear, O Israel, the Lord our God, the Lord is one. Love the Lord your God with all your heart and with all your soul and with all your mind and with all your strength.' The second is this: 'Love your neighbor as yourself. 'There is no commandment greater than these." Mark 12:29-31

Loving God, your neighbor, and yourself, is all one and the same. You can't love one without loving the other. We must not seek for self only or in any manner set self beyond or above any individuals and especially above God. This is what happened to Moses and Aaron, in their anger when dealing with the people at Meribah they broke the greatest commandment. They glorified themselves and not God. This is a sobering thought for all of us who want to give water to others. In whose name are we giving, ours or God's? You are almost at the end of The Wilderness Steps let's don't blow it now.

STEP 14

Double Anointing | Deliverance

Anointing – *The indwelling presence of the Holy Spirit in the life of the believer.*

Deliverance – *Liberation, freeing, rescue, and salvation*

The Long Way Home

Remember ye not the former things, neither consider the things old. Behold, I will do a new thing; now it shall spring forth; shall ye not know it? I will even make a way in the wilderness, and rivers and desert. Isaiah 43:19(KJV)

Isaiah proclaims we must make straight a path in the wilderness. From a metaphysical perspective, we must establish a pattern of activity that leads us directly to God. This pattern of activity is The Godward Steps. We must build a highway (steps) that allows us to travel from our conscious mind straight through the depths of our subconscious mind to a permanent connection with the Super-Conscious Mind. As we travel the Godward highway, we may along the way uncover suppressed rebellious thoughts and ideas that cause us to take the long way around to reach our destination (The Prodigal Steps). This could cause us to spend more time in the wilderness. However, don't get discouraged just keep moving.

Moses sent messengers from Kadesh to the king of Edom, saying, "This is what your brother Israel says: "You know about all the hardships that have come upon us. Our forefathers went down to Egypt, and we lived there many years. The Egyptians mistreated us and our fathers, but when we cried out to the Lord, he heard our cry and sent an angel and brought us out of Egypt. Now we are here at Kadesh, a town on the edge of your territory. Please let us pass through your country." Numbers 20:14-17

Although we wish to go straight, which is the shortest distance, we may be forced to take a detour of endless, barren miles.

But Edom answered: "You must not pass through here; if you try, we will march out and attack with the sword." Numbers 20:18

Edom (Esau, brother of Jacob) is the outer man, body, or the carnal physical phase of man's consciousness. Kedesh (Heb.) – *clean; pure; holy; sacred; sanctified; consecrated; a sanctuary,* is the inherently pure, sinless, perfect, ideal state that exists in the depths of our consciousness. It is here in this state of consciousness that many of our suppressed rebellious thoughts come to light and are judged against higher ideals. As previously stated, we must meet ourselves. And how is that done? By judgment of our own thought-errors against thoughts that are pure, clean, and holy. All conscious desires must be met and dealt with.

To make a way for the Christ Consciousness, the Temple (body) must be purified. Continual observance of God's Laws will establish a pattern that will bring unity to the mind. Studying the Bible, literally, spiritually, and metaphysically, going back through the pattern of numbers, and teaching The Godward Steps to others will help ensure that we stay straight on our path to the Christ Consciousness. The more we comment these truths to memory the more permanent they will become.

To overcome self, we must undo all of our past transgressions. If you take advantage of an individual, a group or our neighbor expect that group, individual, or neighbor to take advantage of you. With what measure we judge that same measure of judgment will be met by us. We must undo everything that we have done to someone else, in this life or a past life. And this applies in the future as well. And then we wonder why our life was such a mess.

On a special note, it was at Kadesh that Abraham dwelt between Kadesh and Shur (Gen 20:1); it was where the spies Josuha and Caleb, were sent to spy the Promised Land (Num. 13:26); where Miriam, sister of Aaron and Moses, died and was buried (Num. 20:1); and where Moses and Aaron trespassed at the waters of Meribah and was not allowed to enter the Promised Land. It was a busy place.

Our faith (Abraham) finds itself a state of "going round-about" (Shur) cycling between what is clean, pure, sinless and holy (Kadesh) and an unceasing progress Godward. Man's development has always moved in cycles in his apparent evolution. Go back and read Godward | The Prodigal Steps.

With each recurring step, man advances little by little, in some cases very little. When man awakens spiritually his progress is more rapid. You've always heard that history repeats itself, and until we learn from our past errors and undo then, it will continue to repeat. In my lifetime and in the past history of which we have a record I have seen no significant spiritual advancement. This saddens me.

It is true to say that the more we awaken spiritually the stronger our faith becomes. Faith is the unseen God and when we are obedient to Spirit, faith becomes part of our consciousness without special effort on our part. It may seem like blind-faith to the disobedient, but it works out beautifully to those who believe.

It was also at Kadesh that twice the Israelites were turned away and not allowed to pass. They were first turned away because of their unbelief (Numbers 13 & 14) and second turned away by the king of Edom. It appears that the Kadesh stage of consciousness is that part of self that is still selfish and rebellious and not allowed to enter the Promised Land and continues to be rejected.

Miriam (Heb.) – *contradiction; outcry; rebellion; bitterness; grief; and sorrow,* died and was buried in Kadesh. Miriam represents the feminine side of the love quality in a man who is still struggling to free himself from his errors and selfishness so that he may be fully released from all bondage to human limitations and enter the holy land of wholeness and Truth. At the Miriam at Kadesh stage of unfoldment, the individual has yet to overcome bitter, rebellious, sense tendencies and desires. At this stage, the feminine or love side of our soul (subconscious) experiences a higher revelation of Spirit and a deeper cleansing. In other words, "We aren't there yet."

The Death of Aaron

To get around the king of Edom the Israelites traveled to Mount Hor and from Mount Hor along the route to the Red Sea. At Mount Hor the High Priest and brother of Moses died. Aaron represents the executive power of divine law and signifies the ruling power of the intellectual consciousness. Aaron and his sons typify spiritual strength, which becomes the presiding, and directive power of the new state of consciousness. Before we can reach the new conscious state or Christ Consciousness we must declare and affirm spiritual strength, and not animal strength (physical strength) as our own presiding and directive power.

This declaration of spiritual strength is absolutely necessary in the permanency of the body tabernacle.

Hor (Heb.) – *to be high; to conceive; to think; a height; a mountain;* was the mountain of mountains. Hor is a much-exalted thought in man's consciousness. It is here that the ruling power of the intellectual consciousness (Aaron, the high priest), which has become the executive power of the divine law to the highest religious and spiritual thoughts of the individual (Israel) seemingly ceases its activities and sinks back into our subconscious mind.

It is at Hor that our spiritual strength, through our declaration as our presiding and directive power (Eleazar) becomes the directive quality of the higher consciousness of divine law into which we are entering.

Eleazar (Heb.) – *God has surrounded; God succors; God is helper; whom God has helped; help of God,* was the son of Aaron and his successor to the Priesthood. Spiritual strength through the individual's recognition of Spirit as their supporting, sustaining power now becomes the presiding directive faculty of the new state of consciousness.

God told Moses that because of his and Aaron's rebellion against His commands at Meribah, that Aaron would not enter the Promised Land. God instructed Moses to remove Aaron's garments and put them on his son, Eleasar.

I hope you see what is taking place here: as we draw closer to the Promised Land, more and more of our selfish thoughts are dissipating and being replaced by spiritual and enduring ones. The old consciousness (Aaron) is fading away, making room for the emergence of the new consciousness (Eleasar). From the outset of this book, I emphasized that the Bible reflects our personal journey, with each character and location representing a part of ourselves. This is why those who have not undertaken this inner journey, those who have not followed these steps, struggle to comprehend the Bible. To them, it remains something external, rather than a reflection of what lies within.

The Bronze Snake

As the people continued their journey they also continued to murmur and complain. Again, they complained about no bread and water. I'm sure by now Moses was getting pretty annoyed and irritated.

Then the Lord sent venomous snakes among them; they bit the people and many Israelites died. The people came to Moses and said, "We sinned when we spoke against you. Pray that the Lord will take the snakes away from us." So Moses prayed for the people. Numbers 21:6-7

Bitterness always carries with it a bite, as seen in the anger directed towards Moses by the community. When we rebel against life's conditions and curse either God or others for our problems, it triggers 'fiery' forces in our thoughts that act like poison to our bodies. God does not directly send serpents upon humans; rather, it's the rebellious thoughts of humanity that create crosscurrents in consciousness, resulting in a burning and biting sensation that some attribute to God.

The original Hebrew implies that real serpents were biting the people, referred to as "the seraphim," or "the burning ones." Those who were bitten by the fiery serpents (representing lustful expressions of life) were healed when they looked upon the bronze serpent that God commanded Moses to make. Moses lifted it up so that all of the people could see it.

The Lord said to Moses, "Make a snake and put it up on a pole; anyone who is bitten can look at it and live." So Moses made a bronze snake and put it on a pole. Then when anyone who was bitten looked at the bronze snake, he lived. Numbers 21:8-9

The lifting up of the bronze snake in the wilderness can be seen as an imitation of Christ's death on the cross.

"Just as Moses lifted up the snake in the desert, so the Son of Man must be lifted up., that everyone who believes in him may have eternal life." John 3:14

Just as those who looked upon the bronze serpent were healed; we too have the power to heal. The serpent in the Garden of Eden is sense consciousness. I hope by now you are seeing that it is the sense conscious within us that must be lifted to a higher consciousness. Remember we are spiritualizing the body. Sense-consciousness is the lowest of all consciousness.

So the Lord God said to the serpent, "Because you have done this, "Cursed are you above all live stock and all the wild animals! You will crawl on your belly and you will eat dust all the days of your life." Genesis 3:14

It doesn't get any lower than a snake's belly!

Desire and sensation are external expressions and not a part of the source of life – Spirit. When we realize that life is Spirit then the healing begins. This is illustrated by Moses lifting the bronze serpent in the wilderness. When we realize the truth about life and lift our thoughts to a higher understanding then our minds and bodies will be cleansed of all falsehood. This is what it truly means to believe in Christ Jesus. False beliefs, limitations, and dis-ease do not exist in the higher Christ Consciousness.

We have the power to heal ourselves if we only believe that the power lies within. Eventually, like all spiritual symbols, the bronze snake was misunderstood. Today, the bronze serpent around a pole is a symbol of the medical field, representing external healing rather than internal healing.

Balaam

Balam (Heb.) – lord of the people; destruction of the people; a pilgrim; a foreigner; a stranger

The Israelites traveled to the plains of Moab and camped along the Jordon River very close to the Promised Land (Numbers 22). Balak, son of Zippor and king of the Moabites, saw how the Israelites destroyed the Canaanites, the Amorites, and Bashan because they wouldn't allow the Israelites to pass through their land (Numbers 21). Balak was so afraid that the Israelites intended to invade his territory that he sought the protection of a Midianite soothsayer and prophet by the name of Balaam to pronounce a curse upon the Israelites.

Balak believed if Balaam pronounced a curse, the very worst misfortune would fall upon the Israelites, and he would be able to defeat them.

Balak (Heb.) – *emptier; waster; spoiler; devastator; destroyer;* represents an empty, void, destructive, wasting, thought that rules the carnal mind.

So Balak son of Zippor, who was king of Moab at that time, sent messengers to summon Balaam son of Beor, who at Pethor, near the River [Euphrates], in his native land. Balak said, "A people have come out of Egypt; they cover the face of the land and have settled next to me. Now come and put a curse on these people because they are too powerful for me. Perhaps then I will be able to defeat them and drive them out of the country. For I know that those you bless are blessed, and those you curse are cursed." Numbers 22:4-6

Moab (Heb.) – *seed of the father; flowing from the father; of his father,* signifies the carnal mind lustful, depraved, and wicked. It is these destructive thoughts and wicked desires that must be overcome. God cursed the Moabites for their worship of false gods and sexual immorality.

Although Balaam was hired by Balak to curse the Israelites he told Balak that he could only say what God allowed him to say. So instead of doing what Balak had asked of him he listened to the voice of Jehovah and blessed the Israelites which made Balak furious. Although we may try, we can't always have our way with another person. Even if we wish to harm someone, the laws are set. Others may be able to harm us physically, but the only way for us to be harmed mentally and spiritually is if we allow it. During your time in the wilderness, others will try to give you advice and counsel. Let them know that those who know the law and live by the law are rulers over their own destinies.

If those who try to counsel and advise you fail in their efforts to get you to stumble, they may try a different approach. After Balak failed in his efforts to have Balaam pronounce a curse on Israel, Balak evidently was able to bribe Balaam to devise a plan against the Israelites that caused thousands to die.

Speaking to the church of Pergamum, Jesus says to them,

"Nevertheless, I have a few things against you: You have people there who hold to the teaching of Balaam, who taught Balak to entice the Israelites to sin by eating food sacrificed to idols and by committing sexual immorality." Revelation 2:14

Be careful that when temptation comes, and it will come, not to participate in sinful acts. Restrain yourself and do not self-indulge. During The Wilderness Steps many tests will come and how you pass these tests will depend on how long you will have to keep wandering in the wilderness.

While Israel was staying in Shittum, the men began to indulge in sexual immorality with Moabite women, who invited them to the sacrifices to their gods. The people ate and bowed down before these gods. So, Israel joined in worshipping the Baal of Peor. And the Lord's anger burned against them. Numbers 25:1-3

Thousands of Israelite men were drawn into the Moabite camp by the Moabite women where they wantonly broke the laws and moral code as given to Moses by God. The whole of Israel was affected by this immoral conduct. The Lord said to Moses to kill all of the participants in this lude behavior.

So Moses said to the Judges of Israel "Each of you must put to death those of your men who have joined in worshipping the Baal of Peor." Numbers 25:5

Baal of Peor (Heb.) – *lord of the chasm; yawning place; lord of the opening,* was an idol worshipped by the Moabites and Midianites during obscene ceremonies. Baal of Peor represents the exaltation of sensuality.

I would like to point out here that selfishness is not the only thing that is being dealt with. All of The Prodigal Steps are always in play, and this includes Step 5 – Sensuality. The

Prodigal Steps are always going to be a part of life, or at least until we leave this density. Self-will, Selfishness, Separation, and Sensuality all lead to Spiritual Destruction, Self-Abasement, and Starvation. If one is present, then the others are as well. So don't only focus on Selfishness alone or you will get blindsided by the others. Until you have committed yourself one hundred percent to God's Will your self-will is always present.

After Moses told the Israelite judges to put to death anyone of their men who had joined in the worship of Baal of Peor, an Israelite man brought a Midianite woman to his tent right in front of the assembly of Israel and Moses. When Phinehas, son of Eleazar, the grandson of Aaron saw this, he left the assembly, took a spear in his hand, followed the Israelite into the tent, and drove the spear through both of them while they were engaged in the sexual act. This action stopped the plague that was upon them by their immoral behavior, but those who died in the plague numbered 24,000 (Numbers 25).

Phineas (Heb.) – *mouth of the serpent; oracle; prophecy of mouth; brazen faced; bold; unabashed,* metaphysically is spiritual revelation and power *(oracle, mouth of prophecy).* It is necessary for our thoughts that are awakening to spiritual revelation and power to be disciplined and directed intelligently in all their ways. If these thoughts become lifted up in <u>spiritual pride</u> or become selfish and act on a purely material plane because of listening to our outer sense wisdom *(mouth of the serpent),* they become all that is signified by *mouth of brass, brazen faced, bold, unabashed,* and are harsh, shameless, insolent, presumptuous.

It may have seemed bold the killing of two people in the name of God, yet at this time and circumstance, it was what was needed to restore order and to prevent the complete dissolution of Israel. It may seem harsh by today's standard but sometimes it is necessary for one or two to bear the punishment for the sin of thousands. Look at the sacrifice of Jesus for example. Remember times were different in those days that's why the

Old Testament was all about punishment. The Old Testament is the spiritually working out of the body-consciousness and sometimes all the body understands is pain and suffering. This pain and suffering will eventually end when we reach the Christ Consciousness as it was love and forgiveness that was taught by Christ Jesus.

During our wilderness journey if we allow our self-will to take over, even for a moment, and indulge in sensuality it will lead to the next Prodigal Step – Spiritual Destruction or to disturbing conditions in our life. So, it's best to keep moving Godward. Feeding our senses, however gratifying will result in a major setback on our way to the Promised Land.

The Census

At this time, it may be a good place to stop and take a survey of your life to see how far you have come and how far you have left to go. After the plague, the Lord said to Moses and Eleazar who was now the new priest, to take a census of the whole Israelite community by family. He was to count all those twenty years old or more who were available to serve in the Israeli army. What is interesting is that when Moses and the priest Eleazar took a count of the Israelites on the plains of Moab by the Jordon across from the city of Jericho, not one of those counted was among those who were previously counted in the Desert of Sinai which took place after the Exodus from Egypt. The Lord had told those Israelites they would surely die in the desert, and not one of them was left except Caleb, son of Jephunneh and Joshua (Numbers 26).

All those who came out of Egypt and murmured and doubted Moses and Aaron were gone. Hopefully, by now, your own murmuring, fear, and doubt have ceased. Remember, the Israelites represent our spiritual thoughts, and all those pagan thoughts that were opposed to and in opposition to these spiritual thoughts are hopefully gone. This was the whole purpose of the Wilderness Steps to purge all the sensual and material thoughts that have been controlling our lives.

The Israelites as well as you are just across the river from the Promised Land so enjoy this time for it has been a long journey. But beware we are not there yet.

The "ites" of Canaan

All of the "ites" that the Israelites had to contend with, the Moabites, the Amorites, Hittites, the Midianites, etc., were all descendants of Noah making them all related. I say this because I want to show you how we all go to the pigpen, and it is there we all have to meet ourselves and the selfish things that we have set in motion and now are waiting to be met by us.

The "ites,"

- Amorites – descended from a son of Canann, grandson of Noah; Generative thoughts that must be overcome by purification of the consciousness, within and without.

- Hittites – Son of Heth, grandson of Ham (son of Noah) – Thoughts of opposition and resistance

- Ammonites – descendants of Ben-ammi, son of Lot (descendant of Shem, son of Noah), Abraham's nephew; wild uncultivated state of consciousness that thoughts of sensuality, sin, and ignorance that have formed in the outer world.

- Canaanites – descendants of Caanan, son of Ham (son of Noah); elemental life forces in the subconsciousness that are under control of sense thought and expression.

- Hivites – descendants of Caanan, son of Ham (son of Noah); Thoughts belonging to the carnal consciousness in man. Refers to the carnal and physical in the individual.

- Perizzites – ancient inhabitants of Caanan (descendants of the Phoenicians, offspring of Sidon, the first son of Canaan who was the son of Ham, who was a son of Noah); the elemental life forces in the organism, only elevated to a more exalted plane by the outer, personal man, and more strongly entrenched in the sense consciousness of the individual.

Notice that most of the "ites" were descended from Ham. Ham is the second son of Noah. When Ham saw his father drunk and naked, Noah felt so humiliated that he put a curse on Ham's son Caanan, condemning his descendants to perpetual slavery (Genesis 9:24-27). I guess what they were a slave to were their own selfish desires.

You can see why God told Moses to destroy all of these people for they represent the sense-thoughts in man's consciousness. Remember Sensuality leads to Spiritual Destruction. Caanan was The Promised Land given to the Israelites by God. Caanan means *lowland,* that is, the body-consciousness. It is in the body-consciousness that the "ites" and sense consciousness exist.

The body-consciousness must be "redeemed" or regained possession of before being allowed to enter the Promised Land and when the individual rediscovers this lost domain all the promises of Scripture will be fulfilled.

Man must eventually possess an immortal body. To redeem his body-consciousness man must enter with his spiritual thoughts (Israelites) into his organism and teach it the saving Truth. Caanan also refers to our subconsciousness. Metaphysically it represents humbleness and receptivity. The land of Canaan also represents the unlimited elemental forces of Being in which man is placed and to which he gives character through faith in God as omnipresent Spirit.

The Midianites

Midian (Heb.) – *rule; government; judgment; subjugation; striving; contending; pleading; strife; contention.*

The Midianites were descendants of Midian, Abraham's son by Keturah which represents discrimination or judgment in sense consciousness.

One of the hardest things for most people to eliminate from their life is "strife." Strife is angry or bitter disagreement over fundamental issues. The Midianites *(strife)* were one of if not the main oppressors of the Children of Israel. They were constantly disagreeing *(contention)* with the leadership of Moses and Aaron. Instead of waiting for Moses to return from his meeting with God on the mount, they took it upon themselves to create a false image to worship. When we create for ourselves false images, false standards are established. This creates strife in our lives as to what is false and what is true. The one trying to oppress the other and the other trying to conquer the other *(subjugation)*.

Petty quarrels, jealousies, and uncharitable thoughts like the Midianites keep showing up as strife in our lives. The only way to overcome these thoughts is through pure love. Strife and contention like the Midianites must be completely eliminated from our life before we can possess the Promised Land.

The Lord said to Moses, "Take vengeance of the Midianites for the Israelites. After that, you will be gathered to your people." Numbers 31:1-2

Moses told the people to arm themselves and go to war with the Midianites. They fought against the Midianites as God had commanded and killed every man. Their towns and camps were burned, and all their possessions were taken including their animals, women, and children. Moses was angry with the officers of the army because they had allowed the women and children to live. It was the Midianite women who caused the Israelite men to worship their idol which resulted in a plague that struck the Lord's people. Moses instructed them to kill all the boys and every woman who had slept with a man. Only the virgin women and small female children were spared (Numbers 31).

Because of the attempt by the Midianites to corrupt and undermine the morale of the Israelites, they were almost entirely destroyed. Even the material gains that Baalam received from Balak for his part in the uprising were temporary as he was reported to be among the dead (Numbers 31:8).

Jesus said to his disciples: "Things that cause people to sin are bound to come, but woe to that person through whom they come. It would be better for him to be thrown into the sea with a millstone tied around his neck than for him to cause one of these little ones to sin. So watch yourselves." Luke 17:2-3

STEP 15

Reprieve | Mercy, Rest

Reprieve – *Cancel or postpone the punishment of someone, especially someone condemned to death.*

Mercy, Rest – *Compassion or forgiveness shown toward someone whom it is within one's power to punish or harm, cease work to relax or recover strength.*

Crossing the Jordan

Jordan (Heb.) – *the descender; the descending one; the south flowing; flowing down abundantly; dispenser from above; flowing (river) of judgment.*

On the plains of Moab by the Jordon across from Jericho the Lord said to Moses,

"Speak to the Israelites and say to them; When you cross the Jordan into Caanan, drive out all the inhabitants of the land before you. Destroy all their carved images and their cast idols and demolish all their high places. Take possession of the land and settle in it, for I have given you the land to possess..." Numbers 33:50-53

The Lord goes on to say,

"But if you do not drive out the inhabitants of the land, those you allow to remain will become barbs in your eyes and thorns in your sides. They will give you trouble in the land where you will live. And then I will do to you what I plan to do to them." Numbers 33:55-56

There is a stream of thoughts constantly flowing through the sub-consciousness made up of thoughts that are good, bad, and indifferent which is typified by the Jordan River. The Jordan River is the largest most noted river in Palestine. The Jordon River is the life flow of thought through the individual from their head to their feet *(the south flowing)*. In the unredeemed and regenerative state, it is muddy with sense concepts and turbulent with materialism.

These conflicting, disorderly, and confusing thoughts must be crossed over by our spiritual thoughts (Israelites) before our true, real thoughts can enter into the divine substance and life in our sub-consciousness. If these turbulent thoughts are not met and eliminated from mind it will be as the Lord said, *'barbs in your eyes and thorns in your sides'.*

You have made it through The Wilderness Steps and now it is time to ponder what you have learned about yourself, about others and about God. This is a welcomed time of rest. It has been a very long journey from the The Prodigal Steps to now and there is a lot of things to be considered. Like the children of Israel, I too wandered in the desert for over forty years. But when I made it to this point, I can say without hesitation that it was a time of rest. I had found the truths I was looking for and Spiritually I felt I was in a good place.

However, don't get too comfortable you still have to cross the Jordan River. Each time we cross water we arrive in a higher consciousness of understanding. Across the river there are more trials and tribulations ahead, but with this higher understanding the suffering will be less intense. I discovered that it was the flesh that was causing most if not all of my worry and fears. Once I overcame the flesh and subdued my sense consciousness, I had less to worry about and found that all my needs were taken care of. Once I got myself out of the way the gifts that had been prepared for me came to me.

(Jesus said), "Therefore, I tell you, do not worry about your life, what you will eat or drink; or about your body, what you will wear. Is not life more important than food, and the body more important than clothes? Look at the birds of the air; they do not sow or reap or store away in barns, and yet your heavenly Father feeds them. Are you not much more valuable than they? Who of you by worrying can add a single hour to his life." Matthew 6:25-27

In the opening chapters of the book of Deuteronomy, Moses recounts what the Israelites had endured during the Exodus from Egypt to their time spent in the wilderness. For "Israel" the one who has striven with God, with man, as well as with self and has now prevailed. That includes you as well.

The following are some of the things to remember and never forget and are for the one who is entering The Promised Land Steps only. These are not for those who have not completed The Wilderness Steps. Far too often we want to jump to the head of the line. This is not one of those times. Each of these "steps" must be completed before entering the new consciousness or else what we have worked so hard to leave behind in the wilderness will follow us to the next level creating a major stumbling block on our way Godward.

Things to remember:

- Rebellion – Do not murmur and complain to God and others about things that you worry and fear when it was you who created the worry and fear that you were experiencing.

- Idol worship – Do not become corrupt and make for yourself an idol, an image of any shape, whether formed like a man, woman, or animal.

- Heavenly Array – When you look up at the sky and see the sun, moon, and the stars, do not be enticed into bowing down to them and worshipping things the Lord your God has apportioned to everyone under heaven.

- Covenant – Obey God's commandments.

- The Lord is God – the things that you witnessed during these steps were shown to you so that you might know that the Lord is God; besides Him there is no other.

- The Law – remember God laws; the ten commandments, you reap what you sow, with what measure you judge that same measure will be judged upon you.

- Walk with God – Do not turn aside to the right or to the left. Walk in the way that God has commanded you and NEVER LOOK BACK!

- God is One – "Hear, O Israel: The Lord our God, the Lord is one." Remember you are Israel.

- Love God – With all your heart, all your strength and with all your soul, love God first.

- Share with others – Share with others what you have experienced and what you have learned. Teach them the steps that you have followed and that they too are to follow.

- False gods – Do not follow the gods around you, the gods that others follow. Remember those who have not made it through The Prodigal Steps are still meeting themselves. Don't let them drag you back to the pigpen.

- Fear God – Do what is right and good in the eyes of God and serve Him only. Do not test God; keep His commands, decrees, and stipulations.

- The Land of Slavery – Remember once you were a slave to the world, to the flesh, to self-will and it was following the steps of God that delivered you from your enemies.

Your time in the wilderness was a time to test you to know what is in your heart. It was a time to humble you. I guess that is why it takes forty years, humility doesn't come easy. For me, humility was one of the hardest lessons I learned. I had a giant ego but following the steps made me realize that my worst enemy was me.

God, through Moses, told the Israelites that before He brought them into the Promised Land, He would drive out all the "ites" that possessed the land. By you Israel, eliminating these false thoughts, the Hittites, Girgashites, Amorites, Canaanites, Perizzites, Hivites, and Jebusites, from your consciousness they will not be projected ahead of you to meet.

Israel was told to defeat all of the "ites" and totally destroy them. Generative thoughts, thoughts of opposition and resistance, thoughts of sensuality, sin, and ignorance, outer personal thoughts, and most of all selfishness must be defeated and destroyed and only you can do this. If you don't overcome them, they will be lying in wait for you down the road.

Hear, O Israel. You are about to cross the Jordon to go in and disposes nations greater than you, with large cities that have walls up to the sky. The people are strong and tall – Anakites! You know about them and have heard it said: "Who can stand up against the Anakites?" Deuteronomy 9:1-2

The Anakites

The Anakites were descendants of Anak (Heb.) – *long-necked; giant,* son of Arba, a giant. Anak symbolizes the belief that the intellect functioning in material thought is the seat of power and the source of Truth. This belief is "giant" in the individual who is unawaken spiritually. This causes them to be bold and brazen *(long-necked)* in exalting their personality. They think that meekness and humility in Spiritual Truth are foolish and a sign of weakness.

The Anakites of today are those who believe that the outer world, formed world, with its customs and teachings, is the real source of man's strength and power. Instead, they see no good in the world and don't understand that the outer world is just a manifestation and expression of man's inner thoughts and of itself has no sustaining power.

It is these types of people, the Anakites, that you will have to face in the Promised Land. It is these "long-necked" people that you have had to contend with all of your life. Those who have bullied you and have defeated and enslaved you. What you must understand is that the world that God created in the beginning is the Promised Land. It has been taken over by false thoughts and beliefs. It is ruled by materialism and the senses (the "ites') and it's time to take it back. This was why God commanded Adam (Sons of God), in the beginning, to subdue the earth and have dominion over it. The early thought-forms had corrupted the earth and had control over it and now it was time to take it back and restore it to its original beauty. The Sons of God (Adam) failed to do this and now it is up to us to possess the Promised Land.

Now I hope you are starting to understand the purpose of The Godward Steps. They are to deliver you from the chains of materialism and empower you spiritually so that what is ours will be returned to us. Here in America, some politicians have campaigned on the slogan "Make America Great Again," but we need to be saying "Make the Earth Great Again." To do this we must circumcise our hearts, be humble, and not be stiff-necked – prideful, stubborn, and uncompromising.

But the land you are crossing the Jordan to take possession of is a land of mountains and valleys, that drinks rain from heaven. It is a land the Lord your God cares for; the eyes of the Lord your God are continually on it from the beginning of the year to the end. Deuteronomy 11:11-12

The teaching and training of The Godward Steps is so that when you reenter the world you will hold fast to your beliefs and not be enticed to turn away and again worship materialism and bow down to it.

Mount Gerizim and Mount Ebal

God has set before you today a blessing and a curse. If you obey God, you will be blessed but if you disobey you will be cursed. When the Israelites entered the Promised Land half of them were instructed to proclaim on Mount Gerizim the blessings and the other half were to proclaim the curses on Mount Ebal.

The Blessing

Mount Gerizim (Heb.) – *shorn places; waste places; barren deserts; rocky places,* represents in those who think and act in harmony with divine law and divine principle. This is a blessing to those who are aware of all that is good – life, health, peace, and joy and understand the reason we have these things is because we are obedient to God. By establishing the good we cut out error and bring life to our waste places, our barren deserts and rocky places.

The Curse

Mount Ebal (Heb.) – *stripped of all covering; bare; naked; barren; stone,* represents in those who think and act out of harmony with divine law in an adverse way. This way of working out errors in sense consciousness results in ignorance and disobedience. It seems hard *(stone)* but it exposes *(bare, naked)* the nothingness of all that does not measure up to the spiritual.

High Places of Worship

Mountains represent exaltation, a high place of consciousness, and a state of spiritual consciousness. The Israelites were instructed to destroy completely all the places on the high mountains and hills where the nations they were dispossessing worshipped their gods.

Mountains are locations for worship and sacrifices and represent obstacles and challenges that must be overcome. Anything that is exalted other than the glory of God, such as idols, altars, and sacred places, must be wiped out of our consciousness. This pretty much is all the material things that we worship or give most of our time and energy. Although, we may have to have these things to survive in the world in which we live it doesn't mean that these material things should mean more to us than spiritual things.

Sadly, we use a lot of these things in our worship of God. The place that was set up by God, the place where we are to bring our tithes and offerings, the place where we are to bring our children and families has been infiltrated by materialism. The church of today is the seventh church in the book of Revelation – Laodicea, the rich but poor rich. Materially the church of today is rich, but it is spiritually blind and poor.

Laodicea (Heb.) – *justice of the people; judgement of the people;* is a phase of judgment in the individual, expressing in the personal. It is all about self. This phase of judgment bases its understanding, and its decisions, on outer seeming and intellectual reasonings and not on spiritual Truth. The church is now more concerned with politics than religion. The church is merging the two into one. This is spiritual adultery, mixing the physical and the spiritual. Don't make this mistake as you move into the Promised Land. Don't try to spiritualize that which is physical and material. Stay true to the Truth.

Remember if it binds you, puts demands on you or enslaves you it is not the Truth.

False Prophets

Now that you are more involved in spiritual things you will start to pay more attention to church leaders and their teachings. The internet is filled with so-called prophets and men and women of God who may be wolves in sheep's clothing.

If a prophet, or one who foretells by dreams, appears among you and announces to you a miraculous sign or wonder, and if the sign or wonder of which he has spoken takes place, and he says "Let us follow other gods" (gods you have not known) "and let us worship them," you must not listen to the words of that prophet or dreamer. The Lord your God is testing you to find out whether you love him with all your heart and with all your soul. Deuteronomy 13:1-3

This will be a test to see if you still are obeying God's commandments. Mainly the first to have no other god before God. Once you know the Truth you will be able to discern if what others are telling you is in fact the Truth. Many are deceived because they have jumped to the front of the line and not experienced a spiritual journey and thus are easily deceived. They are the physical body seeking a spiritual experience. One thing to remember is that God is one, and the only one and no man or woman should be worshiped in His place. And this may be hard to swallow but that also means the man Jesus.

Jesus said, "When you see someone not born from a woman, prostrate yourselves and worship him; he is your Father. The Gospel of Thomas v.15

I assume that Jesus was including himself in this statement as he was born of a woman. It is the Lord God that you must follow and Him you must revere. Also, if any of your close friends, family, or acquaintances try to entice you to worship anyone or anything other than God you are not to listen to them.

Large crowds were traveling with Jesus, and turning to them he said, "If anyone comes to me and does not hate his father and mother, his wife and children, his brothers and sisters — yes, even his own life — he cannot be my disciple. And anyone who does not carry his cross and follow me cannot be my disciple." Luke 14:25-27

These are pretty harsh words spoken by Jesus, but I think what he is saying is that nothing or no one should keep you from obeying God. And that means not putting anyone in your life before Him.

In the Gospel of Matthew, Jesus is talking to a crowd, and his mother, and brothers stand outside wanting to speak to him someone tells Jesus that his mother and brothers are wanting to speak to him.

He replied to him, "Who is my mother, and who are my brothers?" Pointing to his disciples, he said, "Here are my mother and my brothers. For whoever does the will of my Father in heaven is my brother and sister and mother." Matthew 12:46-50

But you say, one of the Ten Commandments is to honor your father and mother. That is if they are honorable. You may honor them as people but avoid being entangled in whatever they do that is not honorable. Follow what Jesus is saying, only those who do the Will of God are the only ones to be considered family.

There are many preachers today preaching prosperity, but they do so only to justify the enormous wealth that they have accumulated from their followers. Don't fall into this trap. God will destroy all those who have enticed others to follow them instead of following God.

You must not worship the Lord your God in their way, because in worshiping their gods, they do all kinds of detestable things the Lord hates. They even burn their sons and daughters in the fire of sacrifices to their gods. See that you do all I command you; do not add to it or take away from it. Deuteronomy 12:31-32

Stay true to God and others and you will always be true to yourself.

Joshua – ego

Joshua (Heb.) – *Jehovah is salvation; Jah is savior; Jehovah is deliverer; whom Jehovah makes triumphant; Jehovah is victory; Jah makes rich.*

It is time for the Moses-ego to leave us and a new ego to emerge. The Moses-ego was to draw you out of Egypt (the flesh) but a new ego, one that is a warrior is needed to possess the Promised Land.

Joshua was the son of Nun and the leader of Moses' army. In Hebrew, the name Jeshua or Joshua is identical to the Greek name – Jesus. Joshua was one of the two spies who gave a good report of the Promised Land. Both of these names are derived from the word Jehovah, meaning "I AM THAT I AM." The only difference between the two names is the extent of realization of the I AM or Christ in consciousness.

Each name finds its power in the I AM or indwelling Christ. The higher the understanding the more greatly increased is this power. It was this power in Joshua that led the Israelites into the Promised Land. It is the power of the Christ within us that we attain and lay hold of redemption of our life forces. This is why scripture says I can do all things through Christ.

I know what it is like to be in need, and I know what it is like to have plenty. I have learned the secret of being content in any and every situation, whether well fed or hungry, whether living in plenty or in want. I can do everything through him who gives me strength. Philippians 4:12-13

The leadership was passed to Joshua because he had been under instruction, encouragement and nurturing of Moses. Moses taught Joshua to accomplish God's plans and move the Israelites toward maturity in God.

And that is a great statement which you may use on your spiritual journey when they ask you what does "Godward" mean?" Godward is moving toward maturity in God.

When we know the law of spiritual demonstration and have the courage to act, this is the Joshua-ego. When Joshua took command, he told the people that they would enter the Promised Land in three days. Joshua was not going to waste any more time. This being said it is time now for you to act. It is time to leave our Moses-ego behind, assume the Joshua-ego and cross the Jordon into the Promised Land. It is the I AM, the indwelling Christ that governs and controls the activity of thought in the inner realm and it commands us to move Godward.

Entering the Promised Land is entering spiritual realization. You may not have realized it before but now you realize that all that exists, all that is reality and all that is eternal is Spirit. By having faith in Spirit as our only reality and by gaining spiritual understanding we joyously enter the Promised Land. When spiritual understanding is established in our mind and thoughts, and we harmonize with divine standards a new state of consciousness is set up called the Promised Land.

Joshua's mission was twofold. He was to bring Israel into the realization of their inheritance and once they were brought up into this consciousness, they were sent forth to take possession of the land. I guess you can say that I've had the same mission. To make you understand who you really are, and where you really came from, and help you to possess your divine inheritance.

Going forward we all should seek to avoid being drawn back into materialism, like the Israelites, we must daily keep our increasing creative power in harmony with our developing spiritual consciousness. But we must be careful we have not yet reached the Christ Consciousness it is still in development.

If we use our developing spiritual powers in an ignorant way (worship of Baal) we may be swept back into Egypt or darkness. Don't forget who it was that delivered you out of Egypt. Those who have learned to trust God, to keep their face turned toward the light regardless of how they are perceived by others, like crossing the Jordon River, pass from one state of consciousness to another *(from glory to glory)* with little or no disturbance.

The secret things belong to God, but the things revealed belong to us. Persisting to go your own way leads to the pigpen and disaster. We are cursed if after following the steps turn away to worship other gods, but offered a blessing if we will only continue to follow God.

This day I call heaven and earth as witness against you that I have set before you life and death. Now choose life, so that you and your children may live and that you may love the lord your God, listen to his voice, and hold fast to him. For the Lord is your life, and he will give you many years in the land he swore to give to your fathers, Abraham, Isaac, and Jacob. Deuteronomy 30:19-20

As we enter the wisdom center God proclaims Himself to be the Father of Abraham, Isaac and Jacob thus our real Father is Spirit. When we emphasize the observance of divine law in consciousness it becomes the leader of all our spiritual thoughts. We have the law of Moses but now we need the action of Joshua, the indwelling Christ. As the activity of the law wanes it is succeeded by the I AM.

The Death of Moses

God did not allow Moses to enter the Promised Land due to his selfishness. Joshua and Caleb were the only men of their generation that God permitted to go into the Promised Land after their time of wandering in the wilderness.

Therefore, you will see the land only from a distance; you will not enter the land I am giving to the people of Israel. Deuteronomy 32:52

By the end of his life, Moses realized that it was his own selfishness, which prevented him from entering. This is true for everyone; it is our selfishness that is keeping us from the promises of God. Until we purge our selfishness, we can only view the Promised Land from a distance. Why would God reward us for our selfish behavior. God makes it very clear that set before us every day is life or death, it is our choice.

Now what I am commanding you today is not to too difficult for you or beyond your reach. It is not up in heaven, so that you have to ask, "Who will ascend into heaven to get it and proclaim it to us so we may obey it?" Nor is it beyond the sea, so that you have to ask, "Who will cross the sea to get it and proclaim it to us so we may obey it." No, the word is very near you; it is in your mouth and in your heart so you may obey it. See, I set before you today life and prosperity, death and destruction. For I command you today to love the Lord your God, to walk in his ways, and to keep his commands, decrees and laws; then you will live and increase, and the Lord your God will bless you in the land you are entering to possess. Deuteronomy 30:11-16

If we don't follow God's commands, He also makes it very clear even if we make it into the Promised Land we will not live there very long.

But if your heart turns away and you are not obedient, and if you are drawn away to bow down to other gods and worship them. I declare to you this day that you will certainly be destroyed. You will not live long in the land you are crossing the Jordon to enter and possess. Deuteronomy 30:17-18

Don't think that someone is going to save you. It is up to you to save yourself. No one is going to go to heaven or across the sea to bring you life, for it is already in you - in your words and in your heart. Jesus' way is the only way; what has been done in error must be undone. And the only one who can undo what we have done in error is ourselves. To forgive sin is to stop feeling angry or resentful toward the one who sinned, but to undo that sin is to cancel or reverse its effects or results as if it never happened. The best way I know to undo a mistake or error is to replace it with love.

Mount Nebo

Nebo (Heb.) – *interpreter; i.e., of the divine will; inspired speech; prophecies; prophet; oracle; height; distinguished; prominent,* represents Divine inspiration, intuition, discernment, foresight.

Moses climbed to the top of Mount Nebo and looked out over the Promised Land that he would not be allowed to enter. Mount Nebo represents understanding expressed on the three planes of man's consciousness – mental, psychic, and soul plane. Nebo pertains to a high place of understanding and perception in the outer senses of the material body. I'm sure as Moses looked out over the Promised Land he had a higher understanding of all that had transpired.

Now that you have completed The Wilderness Steps, you should be more able to discern the spiritual world. Your spiritual development will heighten your intuition and foresight. Knowing The Godward Steps, you will have the ability to understand something immediately, without the need for conscious reasoning. You will be able to "see it coming" before it happens. Everyone and everything follow these steps, thus it will be easy to predict what will happen if these steps are not undone. The outcome is the same for everyone.

"Everyone goes to the pigpen."

No one knows exactly where Moses was buried, and this is probably a good thing. If you know where your Moses-ego is buried, you may be inclined to go back to it. Remember Lots wife; don't ever look back. The trick is to keep moving

Godward. Take the next step and when completed the next step will be revealed.

Like Moses, we all struggle with self-will and egoism. I think you understand now why Self-will and the ego are a major stumbling block to our spiritual development. The enemy we battle is not outside of us it is the enemy within that is the deadliest. We may feel good when we win a battle, but we will not be truly free until we win the war.

There has been no prophet that has risen in Israel greater than Moses. No one has ever known God face to face like Moses did. No one has ever performed miraculous signs and wonders demonstrated by Moses and shown the mighty power or performed the awesome deeds that Moses did in the sight of Israel (Deuteronomy 34:10-12).

The true Promise Land is the spiritual estate we had with God before the world existed. This land was ours from the beginning, but we let our false-thoughts, false beliefs, errors and sins curse the land. True understanding is found in knowing we are at-one with God. The Promised Land is still there waiting for us we must retake it.

Everything we need to possess the land is within us. When we understand that the Lord our God is one and when we become at-one with God there is nothing outside of us that we need to complete our journey home. Then we realize what God said is true, we don't need someone to cross the sea or need someone to descend from heaven to give us the truth that we seek because it is and has always been within our own consciousness. It has been our ego and our selfishness that has kept it veiled from us.

Man is not made aware of Truth through material or material-mindedness the Truth must be spiritually discerned. The purpose of these steps is to move you away from the material world and move you closer to the spiritual world.

Crossing the Jordan

The time has come for us to leave our Pharaoh / Moses ego behind. It is now time to cross the Jordan and enter the Promised Land. Crossing water again is to enter another state of mind or consciousness. We have merged the conscious mind now with the sub-conscious mind the next step is to merge these two with the Super Conscious mind or Christ Consciousness. Instead of seeing things only in the physical we now see material things as spiritual for everything has its conception first in the spirit. The physical is just a shadow of the spiritual. What we see now, this moment in the physical has already happened in the spiritual.

In our material minds, we see everything as physical first and the spiritual as a part of the physical. Most people believe that man was created in the physical (from the earth) and grows to be spiritual. This is a major misconception. Everything existed from the spiritual beginning. Remember the Law of One.

Jesus said, "Adam came into being from enormous power and wealth, but he was never worthy of you (the soul), for had he been worthy of you he would not have died." Gospel of Thomas v.85

The soul is spirit and therefore superior to man despite man being created by God. The soul will not die even though Adam did, and the soul is therefore different in nature than Adam. If the soul is the Image of God and not the body, then the soul pre-existed Adam and like God's immortal image will live forever.

As we recognize who we truly are, everything will be revealed to us. As immortal souls, we have eternal life. Our purpose and our mission are to return to God, our Creator, and live our eternal lives as His companions. However, we must prove ourselves worthy. The only way we can accomplish that is to pass through this earthly plane and rid ourselves of all selfishness.

As we begin to perceive things as spiritual rather than physical, we start to shed our physical self, which we recognize as our identity in the material world. The more we live in the spiritual realm, the less we need the physical. The more we do the will of the Father, the less we act for our own selfish interests. As our physical self is merely a shadow of the spiritual. Then we become that light which we have sought after for so long, and as our light becomes at-one with His light, and His hidden image is revealed.

Jesus said: "The images are revealed to people. The light within them is hidden in the image of the Father's light. He will be revealed. His image is hidden in his light." Gospel of Thomas v.83

Our journey does not end here, there are more steps to take before we reach the Christ Consciousness. Once we enter the Promised Land there are thirty-one (31) kings (usurping thought forces) to conquer before we can peaceably settle down in the land of promise.

In Closing

I hope you have benefited from my books and from my lifelong search for the Truth. The seeker should not stop until they find, so don't stop until you reign over everything in your life.

I leave you with a passage from the book of Joshua.

But if serving the Lord seems undesirable to you, then choose for yourselves this day whom you will serve, whether the gods your forefathers served beyond the River, or the gods of the Amorites, in whose land you are living. But as for me and my household, we will serve the Lord." Joshua 24:15

The choice is always ours to choose, so choose wisely.

Keep moving Godward!

Larry D. McClure

REFERENCE MATERIAL

Godward | The Wilderness Steps

The following material was read by the author, and the spiritual ideas, facts, and interpretations shared were used as reference material to help the author express the ideas, comments, interpretations, understanding, and knowledge of the spiritual topics contained in this book.

The Law of One

The RA Material by Ra, a humble messenger of the Law of One
Copyright 1984, by James Allen McCarty, Don Elkins, and Cara Rueckert
ISBN: 978-89865-260-4
Published by Whitford Press
A Division of Schiffer Publishing, Ltd.
Used by permission

The Thompson Chain Reference Bible

New International Version
Copyright 1990, by the B.B. Kirkbride Bible Company, Inc.
Scripture taken from the HOLYBIBLE, NEWINTERNATIONAL VERSION, copyright 1973, 1976, 1984, International Bible Society
Used by permission of Zondervan Bible Publishers

The Coptic Gospel of Thomas

Nag Hammadi Library
Nag Hammadi, Egypt
Discovered December 1945

9 798889 228168 3